GOD'S
BLUEPRINT
FOR
SUCCESS

GOD'S BLUEPRINT FOR SUCCESS

Wisdom *from the* Book *of* Nehemiah

RAY C. STEDMAN
WITH JAMES D. DENNEY

Discovery House.
from Our Daily Bread Ministries

God's Blueprint for Success: Wisdom from the Book of Nehemiah

Discovery House is affiliated with Our Daily Bread Ministries, Grand Rapids, Michigan.

Requests for permission to quote from this book should be directed to: Permissions Department, Discovery House, P.O. Box 3566, Grand Rapids, MI 49501, or contact us by email at permissionsdept@dhp.org.

Interior design by Michael J. Williams

ISBN: 978-1-62707-677-7

Printed in the United States of America
Second printing in 2019

CONTENTS

PUBLISHER'S PREFACE

From 1950 to 1990, Ray Stedman (1917–1992) served as pastor of the Peninsula Bible Church in Palo Alto, California, where he was known and loved as a man of outstanding Bible knowledge, Christian integrity, warmth, and humility. Born in the tiny village of Temvik in southern North Dakota, Ray grew up on the rugged landscape of Montana. When he was a small child, his mother became ill and his father, a railroad man, abandoned the family. Ray lived on his aunt's Montana farm from the time he was six. He came to know the Lord at a Methodist revival meeting when he was ten.

As a young man he moved around and tried different jobs, working in Chicago, Denver, Hawaii, and elsewhere. He enlisted in the Navy during World War II, and he often led Bible studies for civilians and Navy personnel—even preaching on local radio in Hawaii. In Honolulu, at the close of the war, Ray married Elaine, whom he had first met in Great Falls, Montana. They returned to the mainland in 1946, and Ray graduated from Dallas Theological Seminary in 1950. After two summers spent as an intern under

Dr. J. Vernon McGee, Ray traveled for several months with Dr. H. A. Ironside, pastor of Moody Church in Chicago.

In 1950, Ray was called by the two-year-old Peninsula Bible Fellowship to serve as its first pastor. Peninsula Bible Fellowship eventually became Peninsula Bible Church, and Ray served a forty-year tenure there, retiring on April 30, 1990. During those years, Pastor Stedman authored a number of life-changing Christian books, including the classic work on the meaning and mission of the church, *Body Life*. He went into the presence of his Lord on October 7, 1992.

—Discovery House

1

A PLAN FOR REBUILDING— AND SUCCEEDING

Introduction

S he was an author, a university professor, and a committed Christian. One day, she began experiencing abdominal cramps. When the pain wouldn't go away, she went to her doctor, who said her gallbladder was probably acting up. The doctor ordered tests to rule out anything more serious.

A few days later, while in her office on campus, Kate Bowler received a call from the physician's assistant. The tests revealed a massive tumor. At age thirty-five, she was diagnosed with Stage 4 cancer. That diagnosis upended her world. "Cancer," Bowler later wrote, "requires that I stumble around in the debris of dreams I thought I was entitled to and plans I didn't realize I had made." In fact, she added, cancer had "kicked down the walls of my life."[1]

There are many circumstances in life that can knock down the walls of our lives, leaving us vulnerable and afraid. Sometimes the harm we suffer is the result of our own foolishness and sin. But life is also filled with perils we did not cause, from natural calamities to cancer. Regardless of whether the walls of our lives have been broken by circumstances beyond our control or by our own actions, God has made it possible for us to rebuild those broken walls. God wants us to have strong walls of protection in our lives. We can find God's plan for rebuilding the strength of our lives in the Old Testament book of Nehemiah.

Perhaps many Christians, if they have given any thought to the ancient book of Nehemiah, assume it has little to say to our lives and our times. Although Nehemiah is one of the greatest leaders and role models in the Old Testament, he is not as well-known as giants like Moses, Joseph, or David. Yet Nehemiah speaks to us across the centuries in ways that are amazingly relevant and applicable to our lives.

In the book of Nehemiah, we discover how to defeat the enemies that attack us from without—and from within. Nehemiah shows us how to build strong walls of moral and spiritual protection around our lives. He shows us how to take the rubble-strewn ruins of our lives and rebuild them into a beautiful, functioning temple of worship to God.

No matter what your circumstances, no matter how far you may have drifted from God in the past, no matter how you may have been attacked and buffeted by people and circumstances, the book of Nehemiah will give you a plan for rebuilding the walls of your life—a plan for success in every aspect of your life.

The End, the Middle, and the Beginning

In 1983, I accompanied physicist Lambert Dolphin and noted Israeli archaeologist Nahman Avigad (author of the book *Discovering*

Jerusalem) on a tour through Old Jerusalem. Most of the ancient walls of Jerusalem were destroyed when the Romans, under the leadership of the emperor's son Titus, laid siege to the city in AD 70. Dr. Avigad led us to the top of a section of wall and said, "I have clearly established that this was part of the original wall that Nehemiah built." Words can't express the excitement I felt to be standing at the site where the events in the book of Nehemiah took place.

For centuries before Christ, the Hebrew Bible contained a single book called Ezra-Nehemiah. During the early centuries of the Christian era, that single book was separated by scholars into two books: the book of Ezra and the book of Nehemiah. These two books belong together and are truly part of the same story. The book of Ezra focuses on the restoration of worship and the purification of the people, while the book of Nehemiah deals with the reconstruction of the city walls in the fifth century before Christ.

The books of Ezra, Nehemiah, and Esther all come out of the same general period of Israel's history—and they appear in Scripture in reverse chronological order. In other words, the events in the book of Esther, the last of these three books, took place first. These events were followed by the events in Nehemiah. Finally, the events in the first of these three books, Ezra, were chronologically the last to occur. So if you want to understand these events chronologically, you should read the books in this order: Esther, Nehemiah, Ezra.

The events recorded in Esther took place when God first began to move in the midst of Israel's captivity in Babylon as He was preparing to return the people of Israel to their homeland. Inspired by the Holy Spirit, the prophet Jeremiah predicted that Israel would be held captive in Babylon for seventy years:

> This is what the LORD says: "When seventy years are completed for Babylon, I will come to you and fulfill my good promise to bring you back to this place. For I know the plans I have for you,"

declares the LORD, "plans to prosper you and not to harm you, plans to give you hope and a future. Then you will call on me and come and pray to me, and I will listen to you. You will seek me and find me when you seek me with all your heart. I will be found by you," declares the LORD, "and will bring you back from captivity. I will gather you from all the nations and places where I have banished you," declares the LORD, "and will bring you back to the place from which I carried you into exile." (Jeremiah 29:10–14)

The book of Esther opens just after the halfway mark of the seventy years of exile that Jeremiah had prophesied. At a time when Israel's enemies were plotting the genocidal destruction of the Jews, God elevated Esther, a young Jewish maiden, to the throne of Persia as queen. Some scholars say that it was her husband, King Ahasuerus of Persia, who is the Artaxerxes of the opening chapters of Nehemiah.

The heathen King of Persia gave the command for Nehemiah to return to Jerusalem to build up the walls of the city. Perhaps that accounts for an intriguing phrase in Nehemiah 2:6: "Then the king, *with the queen sitting beside him*, asked me . . ." (italics added). Why does God include this seemingly inconsequential detail? Perhaps it is not inconsequential after all.

I believe, and reliable scholars agree, that the queen who sat beside the King of Persia was the Jewish woman, Queen Esther, whom God had exalted to prominence by His grace.

In this book and in the book of Ezra, the Persian king is called "Artaxerxes." In the book of Esther, the Persian king is called "Ahasuerus." Neither Artaxerxes nor Ahasuerus are names; they are titles. The title Artaxerxes means "great king." The title Ahasuerus means "venerable father." To further confuse the matter, the Artaxerxes of Nehemiah is called "Darius the Mede" in the book of Daniel—and, adding to the confusion, the Artaxerxes in Nehemiah is not the same Artaxerxes mentioned in the book of Ezra.

While some of the historical details in these accounts may be difficult to keep track of, we'll focus on the aspects of these accounts that are clear, understandable, and applicable to our lives today. We will see that God takes the long view of history—and the long view of our lives. Nothing ever catches Him by surprise. He arranges circumstances and events in order to achieve His long-range purpose.

Under King Nebuchadnezzar, the Babylonians captured Jerusalem in 586 BC. They destroyed the temple of Solomon and led the Jewish people away into captivity. Nearly five decades after the Babylonian exile began, the Persians under Cyrus the Great conquered Babylon. So, as the events of the book of Nehemiah begin to unfold, Babylon is ruled by a Persian king, whom Nehemiah calls Artaxerxes. His queen is the Jewish woman, Esther, whom God had placed in a position to influence the heart of her husband, the king. We can speculate that because Esther was queen of Persia, the king allowed Nehemiah, his cupbearer (or butler), to return to Jerusalem and begin fulfilling the prophecy of Jeremiah.

During the Babylonian exile, a small remnant of impoverished Israelites remained behind in the land of Judah. During that time, the prophets Haggai and Zechariah ministered to the people of Judah, urging them to remain faithful until the temple could be restored. Ezra the priest led an early return from Babylon to Israel and began restoring temple worship in Jerusalem. Then Nehemiah, a contemporary of Ezra, led a later return. Twenty-five years later, Zerubbabel would return with about fifty thousand freed captives from Babylon, as recorded in Ezra.

Why did God reverse the order of these biblical accounts? Why are these three books—Ezra, Nehemiah, and Esther—arranged in reverse-chronological order? I believe it is because God's priorities are different from our priorities. From our limited perspective, it seems as if the events should be presented in the same order in which they occurred—first the beginning, then the middle, then the end. But God is not concerned merely with chronology. He is concerned with impressing spiritual lessons on our minds and hearts.

These three books, presented in this specific order, show us the way out of captivity and back to God. The book of Ezra begins with the building of the temple. The restoration of the house of God is always the first step in finding our way back to God.

Next in line comes the book of Nehemiah. The theme of Nehemiah is the rebuilding of the walls. Walls speak of our need for security and strength. In the book of Nehemiah, we will discover how to rebuild God's security and strength in our lives.

Finally, the book of Esther shows us how God is able to use a fully committed believer to achieve His purpose in history. God used Esther to avert a genocidal plot against her people, the Jews, because she was dedicated to serving God, and she was protected by walls of spiritual strength.

This, then, is a brief overview of these three books, showing how they fit together and why their order in Scripture is no accident, but a demonstration of the wisdom and plan of God.

Reconstruction and Reinstruction

The structure of Nehemiah is simple. The book falls into two divisions. Nehemiah chapters 1 through 6 cover the reconstruction of the wall. Chapters 7 through 13 deal with the reinstruction of the people. These, then, are the two parallel themes of Nehemiah—reconstruction and reinstruction.

What does a wall symbolize? The most famous wall in the world is undoubtedly the Great Wall of China. Built over a period of several centuries, it protected the Chinese empire against invasion by the nomadic tribes from the north. The wall stretches along more than 5,000 miles of frontier. It is much longer than the United States is wide. Because the walls were extremely thick and high, ancient China rightly considered itself safe from invasion.

The walls of Jerusalem were similar walls of protection. Jerusalem was the city of God, containing God's dwelling place, the temple. But after the Babylonian invasion, the walls were torn down and the city lay defenseless. Jerusalem was weak and unable to protect herself as long as the walls lay in ruins. And so it is with your life and mine.

The rebuilding of the walls pictures the reestablishment of the strength of an individual human life. You have undoubtedly met people whose defenses have crumbled away. They have lost their way in life, drifting in the streets of our cities, seemingly without hope or a future. But God in His grace frequently intervenes in the lives of helpless, defenseless people and shows them how to rebuild the walls of their lives.

The reconstruction of the walls of Jerusalem is a vivid picture of the way the walls of our lives, the walls of a church, the walls of our communities, and yes, the moral and spiritual walls of our nation can be reconstructed and restored. Just as physical walls provide strength and protection, moral and spiritual walls provide power and purpose for our lives.

"With Salvation's Walls Surrounded . . ."

You may have heard the story of an eighteenth-century sea captain named John Newton, who made his living in the slave trade. He made his first sea voyage as a cabin boy at age eleven, was forced to join the Royal Navy at age eighteen, was flogged nearly to death for desertion at age nineteen, and was sold into slavery when he was twenty. During his enslavement on an island off the West Coast of Africa, he nearly starved to death. Newton was redeemed out of slavery by the captain of the merchant ship Greyhound in 1748, when Newton was twenty-two.

The story is often told that off the coast of Donegal, Ireland, the Greyhound encountered a terrifying storm. Newton thought he was about to die. In desperation, he called out to God. Moments later, the cargo shifted, causing the ship to stop taking on water—and the Greyhound safely reached harbor. John Newton began reading his Bible and eventually became a minister and a hymn writer.

All of that is true—but it's not the whole story.

After Newton's conversion in 1748, he stopped swearing, drinking, and gambling—but he continued to work in the slave trade. Because of his own experience as a slave, he treated slaves less cruelly than before—but he still treated them as human property.

At age twenty-five, Newton married his childhood sweetheart, Mary Catlett, and became captain of a slave ship, the Duke of Argyle. He later made two voyages as captain of another slave ship, the African. In 1754, while preparing to leave England on his fourth voyage as a slave ship captain, twenty-nine-year-old Newton suffered a stroke. He later recalled, "It lasted for about an hour, and when I recovered, it left a pain and dizziness in my head that continued."[2]

Because of his illness, he resigned from the slave trade and stayed ashore. He later wrote, "During the time I was engaged in the slave trade I never had the least scruple as to its lawfulness. I was upon the whole satisfied with it."[3] While serving as a slave ship captain, Newton considered himself a Christian. Yet he later realized that his initial conversion was incomplete, confessing, "I cannot consider myself to have been a believer (in the full sense of the word) till a considerable time afterwards."[4]

In 1788, more than three decades after retiring from the slave trade, Newton published a pamphlet that shook English society: *Thoughts Upon the African Slave Trade*. It opened with the words of Jesus from Matthew 7:12 (KJV)—"All things whatsoever ye would that men should do to you, do ye even so to them: for this is the law and the prophets." Newton wrote:

> I am bound, in conscience, to take shame to myself by a public confession, which, however sincere, comes too late to prevent, or repair, the misery and mischief to which I have, formerly, been accessory.
>
> I hope it will always be a subject of humiliating reflection to me, that I was, once, an active instrument, in a business at which my heart now shudders.[5]

Newton became one of the most outspoken opponents of slavery in all of England. He courageously committed himself to setting captives free. He mentored William Wilberforce, who led the campaign in Parliament to abolish the African slave trade, and he lived to see the enactment of the Slave Trade Act of 1807, which abolished slavery in the British Empire.

John Newton wrote many beloved hymns, the most famous being "Amazing Grace." His second most famous hymn, "Glorious Things of Thee Are Spoken," contains these lines, which suggest the theme of the book of Nehemiah:

> Glorious things of thee are spoken,
>
> Zion, city of our God;
>
> He whose Word cannot be broken
>
> Formed thee for His own abode;
>
> On the Rock of Ages founded,
>
> What can shake thy sure repose?
>
> With salvation's walls surrounded,
>
> Thou may'st smile at all thy foes.

Throughout the book of Nehemiah, we will see the importance of being surrounded by salvation's walls. This book speaks to us across the ages, and it still changes lives today.

So turn the page with me, and let's begin our journey. Let's discover God's blueprint for restoring broken walls and building successful lives.

2

†††††††††††††††

DON'T DESPAIR—
BEGIN TO REPAIR

Nehemiah 1

Sometimes the enemy breaks through our walls from the outside. But at other times, our own worst enemy is within—our own sinful flesh—and we actually become the willing participant in our own destruction.

A number of years ago, a pastor rose to national prominence. He became a sought-after speaker at Christian conferences. He wrote several best-selling Christian books. But during his rise to prominence, he harbored a secret. While pastoring a church, he had become involved in an adulterous affair.

After a while, he quietly and privately ended the affair. Then he left the pulpit ministry and accepted a position as the chief executive of a Christian relief organization. A few years later, he moved into the presidency of another international Christian ministry.

One day, he opened his mail and found an unsigned letter threatening to reveal his past affair. He decided to take responsibility for his past sin, so he resigned from the organization. Then he returned to the church he had pastored, where he publicly confessed his sin before the church and asked the elders to hold him accountable.

Overnight, he went from being one of the most prominent Christian leaders in America to being unemployed and stripped of his good reputation. He underwent a lengthy period of marital therapy and spiritual discipline, seeking to restore his broken relationship with his wife and family, and with his fellow believers. He later said, "I am a broken-world person because a few years ago I betrayed the covenants of my marriage. I know what it is like to live with a secret. And I know what it is like to live once again in the light."[1]

He wrote an account of his recovery, which was published under the title *Rebuilding Your Broken World*. In that book, he recounts this incident:

I found myself one day in the front row of a Dallas church where I had been asked to give a talk. . . . Frankly, I was in no mood to speak to anyone. But I felt constrained not to cancel, and so there I was.

When the service began, a group of young men and women took places at the front of the congregation and began to lead with instruments and voices in a chain of songs and hymns: some contemporary, others centuries old. As we moved freely from melody to melody, I became aware of a transformation in my inner world. I was being strangely lifted by the music and its content of thankfulness and celebration. If my heart had been heavy, the hearts of others about me were apparently light because, together, we seemed to rise in spirit, the music acting much like the thermal air currents that lift an eagle or a hawk high above the earth. . . .

It was a day I shall never forget. No one in that sanctuary knew how high they had lifted one troubled man far above his broken-world anguish. Were there others there that day feeling as I did? Perhaps they would have affirmed as I did: *God was there.*[2]

When the walls of our lives are broken, we need one another in the community of faith. We need to gather together, worship with one another, and lift one another up. That is one of the central truths of the book of Nehemiah.

When Nehemiah returned to Jerusalem, he had a much bigger challenge before him than simply rebuilding the wall. God sent Nehemiah to Jerusalem to restore the people from ruin and despair. Nehemiah faced the challenge of leading the people in a new walk with God.

Jerusalem is not merely the historic capital of Israel and the center of the life of the nation. Jerusalem is a tangible symbol of a human life in which God desires to dwell. In the book of Exodus, God established the tabernacle as His dwelling place among His people. Then after King David conquered the Jebusite city of Jerusalem, God designated Jerusalem as the city where David's son Solomon would build God's temple—His dwelling place among His people (see 1 Chronicles 23:25–26).

The city of Jerusalem is a picture of God's chosen dwelling place— but it is not God's actual dwelling place. According to the New Testament, we are to be the dwelling place of God. God desires to dwell in the human spirit. That's the great secret humanity has largely lost today—one that New Testament Christianity seeks to restore. That's why the apostle Paul tells us, "Don't you know that you yourselves are God's temple and that God's Spirit dwells in your midst?" (1 Corinthians 3:16), and "To them God has chosen to make known among the Gentiles the glorious riches of this mystery, which is Christ in you, the hope of glory" (Colossians 1:27).

That is the destiny God desires for us, that we would be His dwelling place. Jerusalem is the symbol of that relationship, so the picture we see in the book of Nehemiah—a picture of Jerusalem in ruins—is a symbolic representation of a broken human life, a life that has lost its defenses, a life that lies open and vulnerable to wave after wave of terror and destruction.

Every time you see news coverage of a terror bombing of a Jerusalem bus or café, or a rocket attack by Palestinian forces against the city, or threats of war against Israel emanating from Iran or some other hostile nation, you are seeing a symbolic picture of the spiritual danger we all face from without and from within.

From time to time throughout our lives, we need to pause, examine ourselves, and see if the walls and gates of our lives are strong. We need to ask ourselves, "Is my life truly God's dwelling place? Or have I allowed the walls of my life to crumble, the gates of my life to fall into disuse and neglect?" A good place to begin this self-examination process is in the pages of the book of Nehemiah.

Together on the Outside, Broken on the Inside

The opening lines of Nehemiah tell us that this is the diary of the man God called to restore a broken city and revive a broken nation. Nehemiah writes:

The words of Nehemiah son of Hakaliah:

In the month of Kislev in the twentieth year, while I was in the citadel of Susa, Hanani, one of my brothers, came from Judah with some other men, and I questioned them about the Jewish remnant that had survived the exile, and also about Jerusalem.

They said to me, "Those who survived the exile and are back in the province are in great trouble and disgrace. The wall of Jerusalem is broken down, and its gates have been burned with fire." (Nehemiah 1:1–3)

Nehemiah gives us the setting: It is the month of Kislev (roughly the equivalent of our December), in the twentieth year of the reign of Artaxerxes, king of Persia. Nehemiah, an exiled Jew, serves the king in the citadel of Susa, the winter capital of Persia (the land now known as Iran). A fellow Jew ("one of my brothers," v. 2) named Hanani has just arrived from Judah with the report about the Jewish remnant living in the Jewish homeland. Hanani's report is painful for Nehemiah to hear: The Jewish nation is powerless and disgraced, the walls of the city are broken, and the gates have been burned with fire.

If we view Jerusalem as a symbol of a life that has been spiritually devastated, then it's easy to see Jerusalem as a picture of someone we know—maybe even a picture of our own broken lives. If you are living in defeat today, if you feel buffeted by outside forces, if you feel powerless against painful emotions and destructive habits, then this picture of Jerusalem is probably a vivid illustration of your own life.

Some of us feel devastated by our own sins. We may feel helpless against a drug addiction, an alcohol addiction, a gambling addiction, a pornography addiction, or a sexual addiction. We may feel devastated by our own bitter spirit, an addiction to anger or bitterness, or a judgmental attitude. We may feel devastated by the public revelation of some deep shame or hidden sin—a revelation that has cost us our reputation, our cherished relationships, our career, our future. Like Jerusalem, our walls have been broken by our own folly and sin.

Perhaps your descent into destructive habits began gradually, almost innocently. An occasional indulgence became an unbreakable habit long before you were aware you had a problem. You told yourself you could stop anytime you wanted to—but then, when you wanted to, you couldn't. The walls of your city were broken and you were left defenseless.

Some of us feel devastated by sins committed against us. Perhaps you were sexually abused as a child, and the shame of that abuse has blackmailed you into silence. You don't know how to escape the pain of the past, and you're afraid to speak about it. Or perhaps you've been scarred by some attack against your reputation or your career. Maybe you are unable to move past the bitterness and pain of a divorce or betrayal.

The people around you may think you're successful, happy, doing just fine—but inwardly, you know you're not. The walls of your life are in ruins. The gates of your life are broken. You cannot control your emotions, your memories, or even your own behavior. You may appear whole on the outside, but you're broken on the inside.

That's why God gave the Scriptures to us. We have technologies and gadgets and luxuries that previous generations never imagined—but deep down, at the core of our being, we are no different from the people who lived in Nehemiah's day. The men and women of the past have gone through the same moral dilemmas and spiritual crises we face. And in the book of Nehemiah, God shows us how to overcome these trials and reconstruct our broken lives.

The steps Nehemiah took to restore the city of Jerusalem are recounted in the first seven chapters of the book. They are specific steps, and Nehemiah took them in a specific order. If we follow Nehemiah's plan for rebuilding Jerusalem, we'll discover a blueprint for our own lives.

The Pattern of Nehemiah's Prayer

We find the first step in Nehemiah 1: "When I heard these things, I sat down and wept. For some days I mourned and fasted and prayed before the God of heaven" (v. 4).

When our lives are devastated, the first step we must take is the step of prayer. Not just a "word of prayer." Not a ritual prayer or a prayer based on a formula found in a religious best seller. No, it must be a prayer that comes spilling out of our pain and brokenness. It must be an honest prayer—a cry from the depths of our soul.

When Nehemiah heard that the wall that once surrounded Jerusalem was broken down and its gates had been burned, he prostrated himself before the God of heaven. He wept and mourned and fasted and prayed. He poured out the anguish of his soul before God—and God heard and responded.

Prayer is not a "happy face" sticker we paste over our sorrows. Prayer is not a superficial salve we spread over a deep cancer. Prayer is honesty and deep emotion. Prayer often involves weeping and fasting. Above all, prayer involves facing the facts. It means we tell the God of heaven about the hurt, fear, and pain we're suffering. "My sacrifice, O God," wrote the psalmist, "is a broken spirit; a broken and contrite heart you, God, will not despise" (Psalm 51:17).

In his prayer, Nehemiah gives us a pattern. It is a prayer for brokenness, whether we're speaking of the brokenness of a single individual or an entire nation. Let's take a closer look at the pattern of prayer Nehemiah gave us.

First, Nehemiah recognized the character of God: "Then I said: 'LORD, the God of heaven, the great and awesome God, who keeps his covenant of love with those who love him and keep his commandments'" (Nehemiah 1:5).

Nehemiah describes the God of heaven as "the great and awesome God"—and it's important that we begin our prayer with a recognition of God's greatness and an expression of our awe of him. He is a God of infinite power, infinite wisdom, and infinite majesty.

Nehemiah also describes God as the One who "keeps his covenant of love with those who love him and keep his commandments" (v. 5). This is a recognition of God's faithful and loving character. Our God is not some remote and capricious deity on a mountain who might strike us dead on a whim. He is a God who makes and keeps covenants, a God who loves us, a God who can be trusted and who always keeps His word. He is a responsive God, and He is attentive to the prayers of His people.

Second, Nehemiah confessed and repented of his own personal sins, the sins of his family, and the sins of his nation:

> "Let your ear be attentive and your eyes open to hear the prayer your servant is praying before you day and night for your servants, the people of Israel. I confess the sins we Israelites, including myself and my father's family, have committed against you. We have acted very wickedly toward you. We have not obeyed the commands, decrees and laws you gave your servant Moses." (Nehemiah 1:6–7)

Nehemiah confronts his own guilt and the guilt of his people. There is not a hint of self-righteousness in this prayer. He doesn't try to shift the blame onto anyone else. He says, in effect, "I fall down before you, confessing my sin and the sin of my people, because we have behaved wickedly and we have no excuse—yet we come before you, unworthily asking for your grace and mercy."

The destruction of Jerusalem and the humiliation of the Israelite people is not some random calamity that just happened to befall them. It was God's loving discipline of His people for their rebellion and unfaithfulness. Nehemiah offers no excuses or rationalizations. Whenever we try to justify ourselves, excuse ourselves, or blame others for our sins and failures, we delay our recovery. If we want to be restored from a state of brokenness, we need to face our sin squarely and confess it honestly.

Third, Nehemiah reminded himself of God's gracious promises:

> "Remember the instruction you gave your servant Moses, saying, 'If you are unfaithful, I will scatter you among the nations, but if

you return to me and obey my commands, then even if your exiled people are at the farthest horizon, I will gather them from there and bring them to the place I have chosen as a dwelling for my Name.'

"They are your servants and your people, whom you redeemed by your great strength and your mighty hand." (Nehemiah 1:8–10)

Nehemiah reminds himself that the God of heaven is a God who forgives, a God who redeems, a God who mends broken things. If we will turn to Him, He will redeem us, He will change our external circumstances, and He will bring us home to His dwelling place. He has promised to do so, and He is a God who keeps His word.

In Deuteronomy 28 through 30, God made a prophetic prediction through His servant Moses—a prophecy that outlined the entire history of Israel. God said that if the people of Israel were to disobey Him; they would be scattered among the nations. They would be led away into exile. But if they would turn back to God and acknowledge their sin, He would bring them back into the land. Nehemiah recalls that gracious promise.

We find the same principle illustrated for us in a parable told by Jesus—the parable of the prodigal son and the loving father (see Luke 15:11–32). In that story, an ungrateful son took the inheritance his father gave him and squandered it in a far country. In his brokenness, as he ate the same filthy food he fed to the pigs, the son remembered his father and the home he had left behind. He realized he would rather live as a servant in his father's home then to continue living in the squalor and filth of his so-called "freedom."

This young man said to himself, "I will set out and go back to my father and say to him: Father, I have sinned against heaven and against you. I am no longer worthy to be called your son; make me like one of your hired servants" (Luke 15:18–19). So the son got up and returned to the house of his father. But even before he arrived at the house, his father saw him and ran to greet him with open arms—ready to receive him and restore him.

God has promised that if we will return to Him, He will forgive us and rebuild our broken lives. In his prayer, Nehemiah reminded God of the promise He had made.

Fourth, Nehemiah requested God's help in rebuilding the broken city:

> "Lord, let your ear be attentive to the prayer of this your servant and to the prayer of your servants who delight in revering your name. Give your servant success today by granting him favor in the presence of this man."
>
> I was cupbearer to the king. (Nehemiah 1:11)

Who is "this man" Nehemiah speaks of in his prayer? And what does "this man" have to do with Nehemiah's plan to restore Jerusalem? Nehemiah identifies "this man" in the final sentence of chapter 1: "I was cupbearer to the king." Nehemiah was asking God to move in the heart of the king of Persia.

Now, that is a tall order. That is a bold prayer. Nehemiah was dealing with issues and powers far above his pay grade. A butler's job is to answer the door, announce guests, and ring the dinner bell. Solving international disputes does not come under a butler's job description. But Nehemiah wanted to approach the king for help in restoring his broken nation—and that meant taking a big risk. If the king was displeased with Nehemiah's request, Nehemiah could easily face execution. The only way his plan would work was if God himself took charge of the situation and arranged the circumstances in Nehemiah's favor.

So this is the pattern of Nehemiah's prayer—and it's a pattern we should follow whenever we experience brokenness in some area of our lives. First, remember the greatness and the goodness of God. Second, confess your sin without making excuses. Third, remember

God's gracious promise to forgive and restore those who turn back to Him. Fourth, ask God to help you and to arrange the circumstances for healing your brokenness.

Prayer is always the first step toward rebuilding a broken life. Prayer is the place to begin. In prayer, we ask God to take what is wrong and set it right, to take what is broken and mend it. In prayer, we ask God to forgive us, restore us, and guide us.

The moment we turn to God in prayer, the process of recovery begins.

Rebuilding Our Walls—A Four-Step Process

The first chapter of Nehemiah is so rich in meaning for our lives that I want to go back through these verses and extract a whole new set of life principles from them. As we examine the story of Nehemiah, we will see that the process of rebuilding a broken city—or a broken life—involves four deliberate steps. Let's return to verse four and discover the first step in the reconstruction process: "When I heard these things, I sat down and wept. For some days I mourned and fasted and prayed before the God of heaven" (v. 4).

Step 1 is *concern*. You will never rebuild the broken walls of your life until you are deeply concerned over that brokenness. Many people are living amid the rubble of their broken lives, seemingly unconcerned that they have no walls of defense. They seem quite content to wallow in their sins, their addictions, and their apathy toward God. In fact, their ongoing life of sin or substance abuse or immorality or godlessness becomes a kind of drug that anesthetizes them to their own brokenness. If you try to warn them that their way of life leads to death, they'll tell you they're doing fine, to leave them alone, and to mind your own business.

Until we are concerned about the broken walls of our lives, until we have mourned and wept over the ruins, we will not take steps toward reconstructing the walls. Why should we? We're not even aware we have a problem.

Have you ever taken a good look at the ruins of your own life? Have you ever stopped to ask yourself, "What does God want to accomplish through my life? Am I fulfilling His blueprint? Am I fulfilling my own God-given potential? Or am I living in brokenness? Have I squandered the opportunities God has given me? Have I fallen short of God's plan?" Until we ask ourselves these questions, until we mourn the desolation and ruination we have brought upon ourselves, we will never begin to rebuild.

When Nehemiah heard the report of the desolation of Jerusalem, he wept and prayed for days. His grief plumbed the depths of despair. Yet in the midst of his sorrow over the destruction of the holy city, Nehemiah had taken the first step toward reconstructing those walls. And that first step is concern.

Step 2 is *confession*. Nehemiah offers a wonderful prayer of confession to God, acknowledging that the nation of Israel has forsaken God's law and that God's dealings with Israel have been totally just. Nehemiah prayed, "I confess the sins we Israelites, including myself and my father's family, have committed against you. We have acted very wickedly toward you. We have not obeyed the commands, decrees and laws you gave your servant Moses" (vv. 6–7).

Nehemiah goes on to acknowledge that God instructed Israel through Moses, who said, "If you are unfaithful, I will scatter you among the nations." That is why Israel had been taken captive in Babylon. The second step in the reconstruction process is confession.

Step 3 is *commitment*. Nehemiah commits himself to humbly serving God as the instrument of His will: "Lord, let your ear be attentive to the prayer of this your servant and to the prayer of your servants who delight in revering your name" (v. 11).

As Nehemiah prays this prayer, a plan apparently forms in his mind—a plan of action, a mental blueprint for restoring the broken walls of Jerusalem. Though we don't yet know what his plan is, he clearly has something in mind—and all will soon be revealed: "Give your servant success today by granting him favor in the presence of this man" (v. 11).

As we have previously noted, Nehemiah reveals the identity of "this man" in the final sentence of chapter 1: "I was cupbearer to the king" (v. 11).

So we see Nehemiah following these three steps—concern, confession, and commitment (we will find a fourth step in Nehemiah 2). Nehemiah became concerned about the broken walls of Jerusalem, and he wept and mourned. Next, he confessed the sin of his people. Then he committed himself to the rebuilding project—asking God to move the heart of the king.

Whenever we become aware of spiritual and moral brokenness in our lives, we must begin our return to God through these first three steps: concern, confession, and commitment. And our commitment must be a commitment to action and to asking God to act on our behalf. It's not enough to simply say, "I have a plan; I will act." We must also say, "God, I ask you to act on my behalf," because whenever we commit ourselves to restoring and rebuilding the walls of our lives, there are factors we cannot control. God must arrange those factors for us.

I once met a man at a Christian conference who told me of his life-changing experience with prayer. He worked for a large corporation in the Bay Area of California, and he had experienced significant pressure, stress, and conflict with his boss and coworkers. But then a Christian friend suggested he commit the entire situation to God in prayer, asking God to arrange his circumstances and resolve those conflicts.

As he prayed, his circumstances at the office began to change. One by one, the conflicts were resolved. "It almost seemed," he told me, "that I had an unfair advantage over my boss and the other people at work. I prayed—and God worked on my behalf. He protected me from the office politics. He relieved my stress. Before my friend suggested that I pray about the situation, I had never thought of praying for problems in my business life. I thought of prayer as being only for personal matters, spiritual matters, and family matters. I now realize that God does more than give me strength to endure my stresses and problems—He actually intervenes in those problems to bring about solutions."

That man had discovered a truth exemplified in the life of Nehemiah. Here we see that Nehemiah was well aware of his own limited power to affect events. In order for the walls to be rebuilt, Nehemiah needed a power far greater than his own to act on his behalf. So Nehemiah prayed for God to move the heart of the king.

In Nehemiah 2, Nehemiah appears before the king, and he appeals to him for permission to return to Jerusalem and lead the rebuilding effort. Since this is the very king whose wife is Queen Esther, the king is already aware of the problems of the Jewish people. So the king gives Nehemiah the permission he seeks to return to his homeland and begin rebuilding.

The Artistic Touch of God

The first three steps, found in Nehemiah 1, describe the process of rebuilding broken lives. But there is a fourth step we must take. We find it in Nehemiah 2:

> So I went to the governors of Trans-Euphrates and gave them the king's letters. The king had also sent army officers and cavalry with me. When Sanballat the Horonite and Tobiah the Ammonite official

heard about this, they were very much disturbed that someone had come to promote the welfare of the Israelites. (vv. 9–10)

Step 4 is *courage tempered with caution*. Here, Nehemiah encounters the first signs of opposition—opposition that will plague and obstruct the rebuilding process from beginning to end. So Nehemiah will need to demonstrate courage and persistence in the face of opposition—not reckless courage, not foolhardy courage, but courage tempered with caution.

Notice the names of those who oppose the effort to rebuild: Sanballat the Horonite and Tobiah the Ammonite. Whenever you read about the Ammonites, Amorites, Amalekites, Hittites, Jebusites, Perizzites, Horonites, or any of the other "ites" who surrounded the nation of Israel, you are seeing a symbolic picture of the enemy of God—the flesh. The Bible speaks often of the flesh, the fallen and sinful agency within us that resists the will of God.

Here we see the satanic will of the flesh in action. When Sanballat the Horonite and Tobiah the Ammonite hear of Nehemiah's plan to lead the rebuilding of Jerusalem, "they were very much disturbed that someone had come to promote the welfare of the Israelites" (v. 10). Whenever God's people say, "I will rise up and build," Satan, acting through fallen human beings, says, "I will rise up and oppose." That is why we need courage. When we turn back to God and begin doing His will, the flesh will oppose God's work.

Yet the courage we display must be rooted in wisdom and caution. As we will later see, when Nehemiah returned to Jerusalem, he didn't throw caution to the wind. He didn't immediately start stacking bricks and building walls. He didn't start by rousing the populace. If he had plunged into the project without assessing the situation and making wise plans, he would have fallen into the trap of his enemies.

Instead, Nehemiah began by carefully analyzing the situation. He went out at night, when the rest of the people, and even his enemies, were sleeping. He rode around the walls of the city and surveyed the ruins. He took note of the work to be done and began drawing up his blueprint.

So, in addition to concern, confession, and commitment, Nehemiah exemplified the fourth step in the rebuilding process: courage tempered with caution. These four steps are absolutely necessary to rebuilding the walls of our lives.

Sir Edwin Henry Landseer (1802–1873) was an English artist best known for his paintings of animals and for the famous lion sculptures that stand in London's Trafalgar Square. On one occasion, according to legend, while traveling in Scotland, Landseer stopped at an inn for food and lodging. While he ate dinner, a fisherman at the next table told a story to a friend. The fisherman gestured enthusiastically just as a woman passed his table carrying a pot of tea—and the teapot went flying. Tea splashed on the newly whitewashed wall, leaving an ugly stain.

The fisherman was deeply embarrassed, and he apologized to the innkeeper. The innkeeper, of course, was furious at the damage to his wall. Sir Edwin stood and offered a solution. "I think I might be able to do something with this stain," he said. He went to his room and retrieved some ink and a brush. Then he proceeded to rework the stain into a drawing of a regal stag. Part of the splashed tea became antlers. The bulk of the stain became the stag's body and legs. The artist added trees and the grass of a meadow. When he had finished, the ugly stain had been transformed into a scene of beauty and majesty.

That is what God wants to do with our lives. He wants to take our brokenness, the ugly stain of sin and suffering and sorrow that appears to have ruined our lives—and He wants to use His artistic talent and His infinite creativity to transform our brokenness into wholeness and beauty.

Nehemiah has just taken the first step in restoring and redeeming the city of Jerusalem. And in the process, he has shown us how to take the first step in restoring and redeeming our lives. There is so much more that God wants to teach us from the personal journal of Nehemiah.

Let's turn the page and continue this journey of discovery.

3

††††††††††††††

DON'T HESITATE—
INVESTIGATE!

Nehemiah 2

The English language has numerous sayings and slogans urging us to take action when the time is right. In Shakespeare's *Julius Caesar*, Brutus tells Cassius, "There is a tide in the affairs of men which, taken at the flood, leads on to fortune" (Act IV, Scene 3). Brutus is saying that the key to success is acting swiftly and decisively when events reach high tide, when the circumstances are right and an opportunity presents itself.

In the days when blacksmiths were common, people would often say, "Strike while the iron is hot." If the blacksmith heats a piece of iron in a forge to just the right temperature, the hot iron becomes malleable, and you can hammer it into any desired shape. If you strike the iron before it is sufficiently hot, or after it has cooled, you cannot reshape it. But strike the iron while it is hot and fresh from the forge, and you can bend it to your will.

Down through history, wise men and women have understood the importance of just the right moment, of being prepared to take advantage of an opportunity. Too early or too late, and your enterprise will be doomed to failure. But seize the opportunity at just the right moment, and you'll achieve success.

In Nehemiah 2, we see this man named Nehemiah, the cupbearer to the Persian king, waiting and watching for just the right moment to put his plan into action. He knows he must not act too soon—but he must not act too late either. He must strike while the iron is hot. He must seize the right moment.

As the second chapter of Nehemiah opens, we see that the moment of Nehemiah's opportunity has arrived. He writes:

> In the month of Nisan in the twentieth year of King Artaxerxes, when wine was brought for him, I took the wine and gave it to the king. I had not been sad in his presence before, so the king asked me, "Why does your face look so sad when you are not ill? This can be nothing but sadness of heart."
>
> I was very much afraid, but I said to the king, "May the king live forever! Why should my face not look sad when the city where my ancestors are buried lies in ruins, and its gates have been destroyed by fire?"
>
> The king said to me, "What is it you want?"
>
> Then I prayed to the God of heaven. (vv. 1–4)

Notice that Nehemiah dates the events in chapter 2 as taking place in the month of Nisan of the Hebrew calendar, approximately the same as our month of April. The events in chapter 1—when Nehemiah receive the report of Jerusalem's broken walls and burned gates, and his anguished prayer to God—occurred in the month of Kislev, which corresponds to our month of December. From Kislev to Nisan—from December to April—is a period of about four months.

Why did Nehemiah wait four months before bringing his problem to the king? Certainly Nehemiah had many opportunities to stand in the king's presence during that time. Yet he waited. Why? Nehemiah does not tell us the reason for this delay. But I think it's safe to say that Nehemiah, as a man of prayer, was waiting for the Lord to reveal to him the right time to act. Nehemiah was waiting for the iron to become hot in the forge of God's timing.

So, in the month of Nisan, God spoke to Nehemiah, either through the prompting of God's Spirit or through the arrangement of circumstances—and Nehemiah knew that the time had come. Nehemiah knew that a delay could ruin everything. He couldn't afford to hesitate. He had to act.

God still works this way in our lives today. He still wants us to wait for His perfect timing, so He can answer our prayers and arrange events to accomplish His purpose. We are impatient creatures, and we want our prayers answered today—immediately. So we pray, and we expect God to answer our prayers on our timetable, according to our expectations.

Yet God sometimes delays His answers. This is not because He lacks the power to answer our prayers. Nor is it because He lacks the desire to answer our prayers. God is not cruel, and He is not insensitive to our suffering. He delights in giving good gifts to His children.

The Scriptures teach us again and again to persevere in prayer—to keep praying until the answer comes. Though Nehemiah does not give us any details about the prayers he prayed from the month of Kislev to the month of Nisan—from December to April—there can be no doubt that this devout believer, so deeply troubled over the devastation of Jerusalem, was praying fervently, daily, with a broken heart.

Finally, a day came when Nehemiah stood before the king in the performance of his duties as the royal cupbearer. And on this day, as Nehemiah presented the cup of wine to the king, the anguish he felt within was etched on his face. Day after day, Nehemiah had been able to control his emotions and maintain his composure, in spite of his sorrow over his homeland. But on this day, he could no longer keep his feelings from the sharp, searching gaze of the king.

So the king of Persia asked his servant Nehemiah, "Why does your face look so sad?" (v. 2).

This was Nehemiah's big break—his iron-is-hot opportunity—but it was also a crisis point. Nehemiah was in extreme danger. The king had the power of life and death over all of his subjects, including his cupbearer. And when the king asked why Nehemiah looked so sad, he wasn't merely showing concern for the emotional state of his cupbearer. It was Nehemiah's responsibility to taste the king's wine before serving it to him to make sure the wine was not poisoned.

In those days of totalitarian monarchs, the only way to change the government was through assassination. One of the most common methods of assassinating the king was by poisoning his food and drink. Nehemiah had a dangerous job, and he could only keep his job—and his life—by maintaining a reputation for absolute integrity. Every time the king took a sip of wine, he was betting his life on Nehemiah's trustworthiness. If the king had any reason to doubt the emotional state of his cupbearer, if the king suspected Nehemiah of being uneasy because he was involved in an assassination plot—Nehemiah might well lose his head.

So Nehemiah had every reason to be "very much afraid." Yet he also knew that his moment of opportunity had come. God himself opened this door in response to Nehemiah's prayers. So Nehemiah humbly and respectfully told the king he had received word that the city of his ancestors lay in ruins. So the king asked him, "What is it you want?"

Nehemiah responded to the king's question by lofting a quick, silent prayer to heaven. Years ago, we used to call this an "arrow prayer"—a quick prayer shot toward heaven as if it were an arrow. In the era of the Internet and smart phones, we might call it "instant messaging" or "texting" heaven. In the silence of his thoughts, Nehemiah sent God a quick plea for help and wisdom.

Squarely Facing Reality

Having done all he could do to seek God's will and enlist God's help, Nehemiah made his request to the king. And Nehemiah's conversation at this point shows that he had spent a great deal of time thinking and praying about what he should say in his moment of crisis and opportunity:

> And I answered the king, "If it pleases the king and if your servant has found favor in his sight, let him send me to the city in Judah where my ancestors are buried so that I can rebuild it."
>
> Then the king, with the queen sitting beside him, asked me, "How long will your journey take, and when will you get back?" It pleased the king to send me; so I set a time.
>
> I also said to him, "If it pleases the king, may I have letters to the governors of Trans-Euphrates, so that they will provide me safe-conduct until I arrive in Judah? And may I have a letter to Asaph, keeper of the royal park, so he will give me timber to make beams for the gates of the citadel by the temple and for the city wall and for the residence I will occupy?" And because the gracious hand of my God was on me, the king granted my requests. So I went to the governors of Trans-Euphrates and gave them the king's letters. The king had also sent army officers and cavalry with me. (vv. 5–9)

Notice how tactful and skillful Nehemiah's presentation is. Twice he refers to Jerusalem—but he does not refer to it as the capital of Judah. He doesn't even refer to Jerusalem by name. Jerusalem had a reputation as a troublesome city, a breeding ground for revolution against the empire. Instead, Nehemiah refers to Jerusalem as "the city . . . where my ancestors are buried" (v. 5).

Nehemiah employed the God-given skills of a master psychologist. He understood that throughout the Middle East, kings were greatly concerned about their burial. The evidence of the obsession these Persian kings had for their burial sites can be seen in Iran today, near the ancient Persian capital of Persepolis. There, carved into the mountainside at Naqsh-e Rustam, is a row of impressive tombs. Centuries before Christ was born, Darius I, Artaxerxes I, Darius III, and Xerxes I employed skilled stone workers to labor for decades, carving elaborate tombs into the side of the mountain to serve as their resting place. Facing these tombs, a stone structure called the Zoroastrian Cube kept an "eternal flame" burning in memory of the Persian kings.

Nehemiah understood the Persian psyche well, so when he said, "The city where my ancestors are buried lies in ruins, and its gates have been destroyed by fire" (v. 3), he targeted his message on the king's own interests, tapping into the king's sympathies, and presenting his case in the best possible light.

The king asked Nehemiah how much time he needed. Nehemiah knew that the restoration of Jerusalem would take considerable time, so he gave the king an estimate. As it turned out, Nehemiah would be gone for twelve years. I'm sure Nehemiah didn't realize at the outset that the restoration of Jerusalem would take so long, so the king must have had an extraordinary trust in Nehemiah—and he probably had to grant Nehemiah several "deadline extensions," with Nehemiah probably sending a message to the king at Susa, saying, "The job is taking longer than I expected—could I have more time?"

As we noted previously, Nehemiah includes a fascinating paren-thetical statement in verse 6: "Then the king, with the queen sitting beside him." God does not waste words. This statement about the queen is included for a reason. I believe, as do many Bible scholars, that the queen Nehemiah mentions was Queen Esther, the Jew-ish woman whose courage and obedience saved the captive Jewish people from genocide in the book of Esther.

Other scholars believe that Esther's reign as Queen took place before the time of Nehemiah—but if so, Esther might have been the mother of this Persian king, and the mother-in-law of the queen who is mentioned here. In any case, there is a strong possibility that Queen Esther was in a position to influence King Artaxerxes, either directly or indirectly.

Not only did Nehemiah need sufficient time for this expedition but he also needed security for the journey. These were dangerous times, and suspicions were high among the various provinces of the Persian Empire. In order to travel unmolested through those lands, Nehemiah needed to have the proper documentation.

So he asked the king for safe-conduct letters for the governors of the provinces. Later in Nehemiah, we will see that these letters not only granted him diplomatic immunity but also meant that he was appointed governor of the Persian province of Judah. From secular historical accounts, we know that there was trouble in the province of Syria, north of Judah, two years earlier. The satrap (governor) of the province of Syria had rebelled against Artaxerxes. So the Persian king undoubtedly welcomed an opportunity to place a trusted and loyal servant in the governorship of Judah. In this way, Judah became a buffer state between Syria and Egypt, two nations that were often at war in those days. These political intrigues among the Persian provinces provide one explanation why the king was happy to help Nehemiah in his quest.

Nehemiah also knew that he needed certain supplies only the king's authority could provide. He asked for special timbers to be cut for him from the king's forest. We don't know where this forest was located. Some historians believe it was the cedar forest in the mountains of Lebanon, while others suggest it might have been the forest south of Jerusalem from which King Solomon took timber for the construction of the temple.

We only know that Nehemiah's request was granted. Nehemiah had given considerable thought and study to the question of how to persuade the king of Persia to aid him in his cause. From Nehemiah's example, we learn that in order to rebuild our broken lives, we need to think seriously and strategically about how to accomplish this goal. We have to ask ourselves what we need if we are to complete our quest. We need to assess the steps we must take and what those steps will cost us. We cannot approach such a serious challenge lightly or haphazardly. We need to squarely face reality—then we need to invest considerable prayer and thought in order to accomplish the goal of rebuilding.

The king not only sent letters of diplomatic immunity but he also sent an impressive military escort, including army officers and cavalry. Nehemiah went to Jerusalem with the full authority of the throne of Persia behind him. There's a clear parallel to our lives today. If you want to rebuild your life, you need the full authority of the throne of God behind you. You need God's letters of diplomatic immunity and the military officers and cavalry of God's angels surrounding you. When you are sure you have God's backing, you can proceed with full confidence, knowing that the full power of the empire of God surrounds you.

Years ago, while traveling in Israel, I experienced what it means to have the power of a military escort at my side. I was driving from Galilee back to Jerusalem through the area now known as the West

Bank. Israel was in firm control of the West Bank, and tensions at that time were relatively low.

Along the road, I encountered three Israeli soldiers who were hitchhiking. Each soldier was armed with a submachine gun. I picked them up and drove them down to the city of Nablus, a major population center in the West Bank. Just south of Nablus is the little village of Sychar, where Jacob's Well is located. I asked the soldiers if they would like to visit the site with me. To my amazement, these three young Israelis were completely unaware that Jacob's Well was located there, even though they were stationed just outside the city. They agreed that they would like to visit the site.

We went up to the gate and knocked. It was the noon hour, and the site of Jacob's Well was usually closed at that time. But the Syrian priest in charge of the site came to the gate, and when he saw me along with three armed soldiers, he flung the gate open and took all four of us on a tour of the premises. He rolled out the red carpet for us.

At that point I knew firsthand what a difference it makes to have an armed escort. Being in the presence of well-armed soldiers makes a big impression and commands immediate attention.

Nehemiah arrived in Judah with a full military escort, representing the power and might of the throne of Persia. But as we are about to see, even the authority of Persia could not prevent Nehemiah from encountering extreme hostility and opposition.

In Spite of Opposition, God Is at Work

Next, Nehemiah tells us about the opposition that is aroused in the region as word spreads that Nehemiah is preparing to rebuild the city: "When Sanballat the Horonite and Tobiah the Ammonite official heard about this, they were very much disturbed that someone had come to promote the welfare of the Israelites" (Nehemiah 2:10).

Nehemiah encountered two hostile enemies upon his arrival: Sanballat the Horonite and Tobiah the Ammonite. Sanballat was a Samaritan, an official in the Persian government. He undoubtedly envied Nehemiah's close relationship with the king and saw himself as a political rival of Nehemiah—perhaps even the governor of Samaria.

Tobiah was an Ammonite, an official of the government of Ammon, the country we now call Jordan (whose capital is Amman, a name derived from its more ancient name, Rabbath Ammon, meaning "the king's quarters"). The Ammonites were a tribe descended from Lot, the nephew of Abraham. So the Ammonites were related to the Israelites but were always an enemy of Israel.

The situation Nehemiah faced was very much like what the Christian life is all about. I once heard the word "Christian" defined as "a person who is completely fearless, continually cheerful, and constantly in trouble." We grow emotionally and spiritually as we face problems in the power of God. Through times of trouble and testing, God proves to us that we can always rely on Him to provide what we need in any situation. Nehemiah was about to undergo such a time of growth and testing as he arrived in Judah and prepared to rebuild the walls and gates of Jerusalem.

I once had lunch with Cameron Townsend, the founder of Wycliffe Bible Translators, and he told me how Wycliffe began its ministry in Mexico. This was back in the 1920s and 1930s, after Mexico had largely shaken off the temporal power of the Catholic Church. There was widespread opposition to public preaching and the growth of churches.

Townsend went to a tiny Indian village up in the mountains and began to work there, translating the Scriptures into the native language. Although he was not allowed to preach, he was allowed to reach out to people and offer help. Because of poor water resources and inadequate farming practices, local farmers frequently experienced crop failures. Townsend taught them how to dam up a stream and divert water to their fields. In the process, the farmers greatly increased their crop production and improved their local economy.

Cameron Townsend also showed the people how to establish certain industries in their village that would enable them to bring more revenue to their community. Soon, word of these successes reached the ear of Lázaro Cárdenas, the newly elected president of Mexico. Cárdenas sincerely wanted to help the indigenous people of Mexico. One day the president drove out in his limousine to the village south of Mexico City, and, when Cameron Townsend saw the presidential limousine, he went up to greet the president and introduce himself.

The president said, "You're the very man I came to see." He invited Townsend to come to the capital, and they became close friends for the duration of Cárdenas's presidency. President Cárdenas flung open a door of ministry for Wycliffe Translators, and later presidents continued their support.

God is constantly at work in our lives in ways we cannot always foresee. Nehemiah relied on God to arrange the circumstances of his life so he could carry out God's plan. We need to have the same view of God's work in our lives that Nehemiah demonstrated. If you are struggling with some habit, some painful circumstance in your life, some crisis or problem that seems to hold you down, learn from Nehemiah. Expect God to act, perhaps in ways you cannot anticipate. That's the lesson of this drama for our lives today.

Prepared for Leadership

God has opened a door of opportunity for Nehemiah, and Nehemiah has seized the critical moment. But there is another step Nehemiah must take to rebuild the broken walls of Jerusalem. He must honestly face the full reality of the challenge before him:

I went to Jerusalem, and after staying there three days I set out during the night with a few others. I had not told anyone what my God had put in my heart to do for Jerusalem. There were no mounts with me except the one I was riding on.

By night I went out through the Valley Gate toward the Jackal Well and the Dung Gate, examining the walls of Jerusalem, which had been broken down, and its gates, which had been destroyed by fire. Then I moved on toward the Fountain Gate and the King's Pool, but there was not enough room for my mount to get through; so I went up the valley by night, examining the wall. Finally, I turned back and reentered through the Valley Gate. The officials did not know where I had gone or what I was doing, because as yet I had said nothing to the Jews or the priests or nobles or officials or any others who would be doing the work. (Nehemiah 2:11–16)

Expecting opposition, Nehemiah kept his own counsel. Except for a few close aides, he didn't tell anyone his plans until he could see for himself what needed to be done. He found the walls in such a state of ruin that the rubble blocked his path on the valley floor, and he had to reenter the city by the Valley Gate.

When we face the brokenness of our own lives, we need to be realists. We need to search out the facts as they are, name them, and admit them honestly to ourselves and others. As long as we try to ignore the truth, deny the truth, or shift the blame, we'll remain mired in our problems. Only the truth will set us free.

If you're familiar with the work of Alcoholics Anonymous, you know that the first requirement of an alcoholic coming into the program is an honest acknowledgment of the truth. He must state clearly and unequivocally, "I am an alcoholic." Until an individual is willing to face the truth, recovery will remain out of reach.

Nehemiah personally assessed the extent of the challenge before him. Then, once he had taken stock of the problem, it was time

to enlist the entire Jerusalem community in the effort to meet the
challenge and rebuild the walls:

> Then I said to them, "You see the trouble we are in: Jerusalem lies in
> ruins, and its gates have been burned with fire. Come, let us rebuild
> the wall of Jerusalem, and we will no longer be in disgrace." I also
> told them about the gracious hand of my God on me and what the
> king had said to me.
>
> They replied, "Let us start rebuilding." So they began this good
> work. (vv. 17–18)

This passage is one of the reasons Nehemiah is regarded as a role
model of biblical leadership. No one can rebuild the broken walls
of the city by himself. A challenge this big requires the active in-
volvement of the entire community. It requires a team effort. And
every effective team must have a strong leader. Leadership is the art
of achieving great, challenging goals through other people. Here
Nehemiah demonstrates his leadership ability.

Where did Nehemiah learn the art of leadership? Without doubt,
he learned many crucial leadership lessons as the cupbearer to the
king of Persia. He had seen the king in the midst of making difficult
decisions, in the midst of discussions with his advisors, in the midst of
mapping strategies and making plans. Nehemiah had studied under
one of the great leaders of the ancient world. The years Nehemiah spent
in the court of the king of Persia prepared him well for this moment.

So Nehemiah called the people together and told them, in effect,
"Look around you. See the ruins of this once-great city. See the
trouble we're in. Our nation is disgraced by the fallen condition
of our city. Let's come together and rebuild these walls—and let's
remove this disgrace from our city and from ourselves."

He went on to tell them that the hand of God was with them—
and that the king of Persia was behind them in their efforts to restore

their broken city. God had moved the heart of the king. Now it was time for the people of Israel to roll up their sleeves and get to work.

Bold, godly leadership usually attracts a following. So it was with Nehemiah. He spoke to the people, and he galvanized them to action. They responded immediately and enthusiastically, "Let us start rebuilding" (v. 18). He appealed to their self-respect, and he motivated them to get to work.

A Crab Mentality

Whenever you begin to build, there will always be someone who wants to tear down. Whenever you begin to recover, there will always be someone who wants to deal you a setback. Whenever you begin to make progress, there will always be obstacles and resistance in your path. This principle is true today, and it was true in the life of Nehemiah: "But when Sanballat the Horonite, Tobiah the Ammonite official and Geshem the Arab heard about it, they mocked and ridiculed us. 'What is this you are doing?' they asked. 'Are you rebelling against the king'" (v. 19).

We have already met Sanballat the Horonite and Tobiah the Ammonite—but now we meet a third opponent: Geshem the Arab.

In the 1960s, research psychologist Victor Goertzel and his wife Mildred published a study of more than 400 gifted and highly successful people. They later expanded that study to include more than 700 successful people, and they published the study under the title *Cradles of Eminence.* Looking at all the different factors that motivated these people to become successful in their various fields of endeavor, the Goertzels only found one common thread, one factor nearly all of them had in common: they had overcome difficult obstacles and opposition to become the kind of people they were.

Some had to overcome abusive or domineering parents. Some had overcome alcoholic or failure-prone parents. Some had overcome physical disabilities or childhood illnesses. Some had battled poverty, racism, tragedy, abandonment, or mental illness. Yet it was the very factor that seemed the most likely to destroy them that actually made them stronger. When we have to overcome obstacles and opposition to achieve our goals, those difficulties can actually make us stronger and increase our likelihood of success. God uses the difficult experiences in our lives to increase our strength and intensify our trust in Him.

But we have to cooperate with God in the process of growing through trials. We have to say, "Lord, teach me the lessons you would have me learn through this difficult time." If we ask Him for wisdom and strength, He will give it to us. Trials are inevitable—but learning from our trials is optional. Make sure you choose to cooperate with God in learning the hard lessons that will lead you to success.

Sanballat, Tobiah, and Geshem the Arab have come to oppose God's work and to afflict Nehemiah as he led the rebuilding effort. But Nehemiah would not be distracted by the opposition of these evil men. Instead, their opposition just strengthened his determination to see this project through. When these men taunted him, he was ready with an answer: "I answered them by saying, 'The God of heaven will give us success. We his servants will start rebuilding, but as for you, you have no share in Jerusalem or any claim or historic right to it'" (v. 20).

Nehemiah's three opponents had no part in the covenant of promise. One was a political enemy, Sanballat the Horonite. One was a renegade descendent of Lot, Tobiah, a distant relative of the Israelites, and a man who chose to be the Israelites' enemy. The third was an Arab, a descendant of Ishmael. They were oppressors and bullies. They occupied the land that belonged to the Israelites even though they had no claim to God's promise of an inheritance. Nehemiah could not be intimidated. He told these men that God would give the Israelite people success—and the three opponents would do well to simply go away.

If you have ever tried to achieve something or build something for God, you may be familiar with the pattern of opposition these three men inflicted on Nehemiah and the Israelites. They begin by mocking and ridiculing God's people. You may have felt the sting of ridicule as you have been recovering from the ruins of your own life. People you once considered friends sometimes laugh at your desire to change. If you succeed in rebuilding and restoring your life, it will make them feel bad about their own lives—so they want to drag you down to their own level.

Have you ever seen a barrel or bucket of live crabs at a pier or in a seafood restaurant? Individually, the crabs might be able to escape from the bucket—but collectively, they are trapped by what is known as a "crab mentality." Any crab that tries to crawl up to the top of the bucket to make his escape will be stopped and dragged down by two or three other crabs. It's as if the crabs are saying to each other, "If I can't escape, neither can you." So they continually drag each other down and doom each other to the stewpot.

Let me give you an example of how this principle might apply to your life today: If you try to break free of an addiction, your old friends will be there to oppose you, mock you, and say, "What are you trying to prove? You'll never break that habit. You're not better than us. We are doomed to be addicts and so are you." Like crabs in a barrel, they keep dragging you back to their level, ridiculing your effort to rebuild your life while mocking your faith in Christ. Why? Because if you succeed, it will rob them of their excuses for failure.

Nehemiah's three opponents had a "crab mentality." They didn't want to see the rebuilding effort succeed, so they did everything in their power to oppose Nehemiah's leadership, beginning with mocking and ridiculing the effort to rebuild.

But mocking and ridicule was just the first step. When their taunts failed to stop Nehemiah, they escalated to the next level of resistance. Nehemiah's enemies began to threaten and slander him, charging him with rebellion and disloyalty to the king.

This is a picture of another kind of opposition we face—an opposition that comes straight from Satan himself. Satan is a slanderer. Satan is an intimidator. Satan is an accuser. Whenever we experience a moral failure, Satan will charge us with a crime. He will accuse us of disloyalty to our King, God the Father.

Satan has no say over our lives. Jesus has paid the price of our redemption, and now we are God's property. So when we face resistance from Satan, we need to allow God to go before us and fight the battle. We don't have to listen to the slander of Satan. We don't have to believe anything he says about us. On the cross, the Lord Jesus Christ set us free. As the apostle Paul wrote, "it is for freedom that Christ has set us free" (Galatians 5:1).

This means we do not have to be bound by habits from the past. We do not need to be slaves to drugs, alcohol, tobacco, sex, gambling, or any other habit or behavior that attempts to control us or limit us. Remember the apostle Paul's great shout of defiance: "I will not be mastered by anything" (1 Corinthians 6:12). Why? Because he was under the power of God. This is what Nehemiah declares here.

We don't need to be slaves to fear, to anger, to bitterness, to a judgmental spirit, or to a complaining spirit. These impulses that seek to ruin our lives can be overcome, because we trust in the infinite power of God. We believe that God will grant us the grace to stand.

That is why Nehemiah clenches his fist and says, in effect, "The God of heaven is with us. He will give us success and enable us to prevail over your opposition. You have no part in God's plan and purpose. But we, his servants, will rebuild. Do your worst. You can't stop us. You are usurpers and have no right to this land. We are here by the will of Almighty God. And we will rebuild."

Prophetic Significance

There is a significance to the events we are studying here that you may not realize. There is a reason Satan inspires these three men to bitterly oppose God's program of rebuilding the city of Jerusalem. As we move through the book of Nehemiah, we are going to see this satanic opposition grow in strength and severity. So why is Satan opposing God's work in rebuilding Jerusalem?

Because Satan is fighting against the coming of the Messiah.

In Daniel 9, there is a great prophecy regarding the history of Israel. In that prophecy, God promises that a period of 490 years will be marked off in which God will do tremendous things for Israel. When does the 490-year period begin? In the book of Daniel, the angel Gabriel appears to Daniel and says:

> "Know and understand this: From the time the word goes out to restore and rebuild Jerusalem until the Anointed One, the ruler, comes, there will be seven 'sevens,' and sixty-two 'sevens.' It will be rebuilt with streets and a trench, but in times of trouble. After the sixty-two 'sevens,' the Anointed One will be put to death and will have nothing. The people of the ruler who will come will destroy the city and the sanctuary. The end will come like a flood: War will continue until the end, and desolations have been decreed." (Daniel 9:25–26)

When the decree goes forth to rebuild Jerusalem, God's clock begins to tick. As we have seen, Artaxerxes issues a decree to Nehemiah, the governor of the province of Judah, commissioning him to rebuild Jerusalem, just as the angel Gabriel foretold in the book of Daniel. Following that decree, a period of 483 years will take place—"seven 'sevens,' and sixty-two 'sevens.'" At the end of that time, the Messiah, the Anointed One, would be "put to death and will have nothing" (v. 26). This speaks of the crucifixion of Jesus the Messiah.

Then there is a strange statement: "He will confirm a covenant with many for one 'seven'" (Daniel 9:27). What is this seven-year period Gabriel speaks of in the book of Daniel? We find the answer in parallel passages in the New Testament—Matthew 24, 2 Thessalonians 2, and the book of Revelation. These passages speak of prophetic events that have not yet come to pass. These events will take place during the period of judgment upon the earth known as the Great Tribulation.

All these prophetic events are tied together with the book of Nehemiah in a fascinating way. Here in Nehemiah, we have the decree of Artaxerxes, king of Persia, which sets God's prophetic timetable in motion, leading to the incarnation and crucifixion of Jesus the Messiah. Now we begin to understand why these three opponents, inspired by Satan, have opposed Nehemiah's work with such vehemence and rage. These three men are the human agents of Satan's opposition to God's program in history.

But at the same time, I don't want us to lose sight of the fact that the steps of recovery Nehemiah exemplifies in this book are given for our instruction. Nehemiah is a role model for God's blueprint for recovery. If we follow the pattern Nehemiah set for us, God will lead us to recovery from our brokenness.

Here are the three steps Nehemiah has shown us so far: First, recovery begins with a deep concern that leads to sorrow and prayer to God. Second, our concern and sorrow produces an opportunity for change, which calls us to respond. Third, our response to that opportunity leads us to face the facts of our crisis, honestly and squarely. When God calls us to rebuild, he says, in effect, "Don't hesitate—investigate!" God wants us to respond immediately, to assess the situation, and to honestly admit that our lives are broken and we are in crisis.

When we take these first three steps, we have begun the process of recovery and rebuilding. We are ready for God to move in our lives to help us rebuild our walls and restore our gates—for our good and for His glory.

4

††††††††††††††††

DON'T BE PARALYZED— GET ORGANIZED!

Nehemiah 3

I think reality is overrated," said a character in a recent best-selling novel.[1] Those words express the mood of the times in which we live. All around us, people are making a mass exodus away from reality and into illusion. Many of us flee reality through the abuse of substances such as alcohol, street drugs, or prescription drugs. Or we flee reality by zoning out in front of the TV or by staring incessantly at the screens on our smart phones or computers. Or we flee reality by engaging in pornography or casual sex, taking God's gift of sexual expression and marriage and turning it into a selfish and irresponsible pastime. We are now capable of immersing ourselves in so-called "virtual reality," in which the most startling sounds and three-dimensional images will flood our senses—and I predict that many people will become so addicted to "virtual reality" that they will never come out of their bedrooms or basements to experience real reality again.

There's always a price to pay for avoiding reality. You can ignore reality for a while, but that doesn't mean it goes away. In fact, many of the means we use to escape reality—substance abuse, sexual promiscuity, and other addictive behavior—come with real and painful consequences. By avoiding reality, by taking refuge in illusion, we only compound the problems that await us when we can no longer avoid reality. In Nehemiah 3, we learn how to make our way back to reality after experiencing the destructive consequences of our foolish illusions.

As we make our way through this chapter, we'll find that it contains an abundance of unpronounceable names, and you may find these names a bit foreboding at first—but please don't let these names keep you from discovering the rich truths embedded in this great book. We should be encouraged to realize that God has not forgotten the names of the men and women who labored to restore and rebuild the city of Jerusalem. And if God did not forget their names, He won't forget our names either.

Nehemiah 3 tells the story of the restoration of the city gates and walls, and it shows that whenever we face a daunting challenge, we need the help of other people in our community of faith. We cannot do it alone. This chapter illustrates the need for cooperation and mutual support. It is an Old Testament illustration of some important New Testament truths concerning the body of Christ. As we see in such passages as 1 Corinthians 12 and Romans 12, believers in Christ are part of a worldwide body made up of many members. We belong to each other and we are to help one another and bear one another's burdens.

In this chapter of Nehemiah, we discover four important principles for working together as believers. As the New Testament teaches us, there are two things we cannot say to one another as

Christians. One is: "You do not need me." The other is: "I do not need you." Everyone in the body of Christ needs everyone else. Only when we are fully aware of this truth and committed to living it out does the church become a living, vital, loving fellowship.

As we go through Nehemiah 3, we stand beside Nehemiah as he surveys the destruction of each gate in Jerusalem. Each of those gates can have symbolic importance to us and can speak of a quality of life each of us needs. In Scripture, gates represent access and egress—a way to go in and a way to come out. They represent our ability to enter into each other's lives—and the ability to let other believers enter our lives. Through the "gates" of our lives, we reach out to one another and we allow others to hear our thoughts and share our feelings.

In his second letter, the apostle Peter writes about certain qualities we should add to our lives and our behavior in order to keep the gates of our lives in good repair. He writes:

> For this very reason, make every effort to add to your faith goodness; and to goodness, knowledge; and to knowledge, self-control; and to self-control, perseverance; and to perseverance, godliness; and to godliness, mutual affection; and to mutual affection, love. (2 Peter 1:5–7)

If we follow this exhortation of Peter, we will no longer live unfruitful and unproductive lives. The gates of our lives will be in good repair, and our community of faith will be strong and secure. Let's take a closer look at Nehemiah 3 and discover the life-changing principles that are vividly represented there.

Instructive Principles for Our Lives

In the opening verses of Nehemiah 3, we see the first stages of the rebuilding project, and we see that all the people were involved in the effort:

Eliashib the high priest and his fellow priests went to work and rebuilt the Sheep Gate. They dedicated it and set its doors in place, building as far as the Tower of the Hundred, which they dedicated, and as far as the Tower of Hananel. The men of Jericho built the adjoining section, and Zakkur son of Imri built next to them. (vv. 1–2)

These verses illustrate an important New Testament principle: the ministry of the church belongs to everyone in the congregation, not just the so-called "ministers." The New Testament does not divide the church into two parts: the clergy and the spectators. Everyone in the church is, in a very real sense, a "minister" because every believer should have a ministry. Every Christian should be actively engaged in building up the body of Christ and carrying out the work of the church in the world.

In many parts of the Christian world today, people think that only the pastor and the hired staff members are expected to do the work of evangelizing, teaching, counseling, healing the hurts of others, and serving the needy. Because we have followed this practice for decades, the church is in trouble all around the world. But the work of the ministry belongs to the whole congregation. This principle is illustrated by the first two verses of Nehemiah 3.

In the opening verses of this account, everyone is involved. Eliashib the high priest and his fellow priests began the work by rebuilding the Sheep Gate and dedicating it to God. If you think preachers only work on Sundays, think again. Here are the "preachers" of Nehemiah's day, and they are out in the hot sun, working up a sweat, putting stones and mortar in place, and hanging new doors on the broken gates. This is hard, backbreaking work—and the priests of Israel are setting an example for the people they serve.

As we proceed through this account, we will see that everyone in the city, the rich and the poor, the powerful and the lowly, the priests and Levites, the civil servants and the business leaders, the gatekeepers and the guards, the farmers and the pharmacists, the merchants and the servants—all were involved in the rebuilding effort, all got their hands dirty, all did their part.

Lest someone think the task of rebuilding the city walls was "men's work," Nehemiah tells us that the women of the city were directly involved as well: "Shallum son of Hallohesh, ruler of a half-district of Jerusalem, repaired the next section with the help of his daughters" (v. 12).

What kind of work did the daughters of Shallum do? Nehemiah doesn't say. But it's clear that these women were completely committed to the effort, and they worked right along with the men. It's encouraging to see this demonstration of equality between the sexes even in those days. The account continues:

> The Valley Gate was repaired by Hanun and the residents of Za-noah. They rebuilt it and put its doors with their bolts and bars in place. They also repaired a thousand cubits of the wall as far as the Dung Gate.
>
> The Dung Gate was repaired by Malkijah son of Rekab, ruler of the district of Beth Hakkerem. He rebuilt it and put its doors with their bolts and bars in place.
>
> The Fountain Gate was repaired by Shallun son of Kol-Hozeh, ruler of the district of Mizpah. He rebuilt it, roofing it over and putting its doors and bolts and bars in place. He also repaired the wall of the Pool of Siloam, by the King's Garden, as far as the steps going down from the City of David. Beyond him, Nehemiah son of Azbuk, ruler of a half-district of Beth Zur, made repairs up to a point opposite the tombs of David, as far as the artificial pool and the House of the Heroes. (vv. 13–16)

Everyone involved in the reconstruction project was a volunteer. No one was conscripted, no one was hired, no one was paid. Notice at the end of this section that Nehemiah refers to "the artificial pool and the House of Heroes." What was the House of Heroes? Who occupied it in those days? No one knows. The significance of the House of Heroes has been lost to history.

One time, a number of years ago, I went to San Antonio, Texas, for a board meeting of Bible Study Fellowship, the organization that encourages men's and women's Bible study classes across the country and around the world. In San Antonio they have built a number of apartments they call the House of Heroes. It is used to house the volunteers who come and devote days, weeks, or even months to helping out in the work of that ministry. Their donated effort saves the organization countless thousands of dollars every year, so they provide these "heroes of the faith" with a House of Heroes for them to stay in.

God's People Working Together

Notice too that the volunteers who rebuilt the walls of Jerusalem were not all residents of Jerusalem. Some came from surrounding cities, villages, and regions around Judah—cities like Jericho, Tekoa, and Mizpah.

There is a clear parallel here with the body of Christ, the church. We are all engaged in the ministry, and there are no geographical distinctions or dividing lines. You may have the great privilege of reaching out and doing evangelistic ministry in your own neighborhood. Or God may prompt you to become involved in a short-term or long-term ministry in some distant part of the world. You will find that believers are very much the same wherever you go. When you meet another person who loves Jesus as you do, there's an instant bond between you that transcends all distinctions of race, ethnicity, language, culture, age, education, and economic class. Even if you don't speak the same language, you will love each other and be one in the spirit of God.

The people of Jerusalem and the people from the outlying farms and villages came together, united by their love of God and their mission of rebuilding the holy city. We need to recapture that spirit of unity and common purpose in the church today. We need to understand that each of us has a ministry in the church; each of us has a purpose to fulfill. We should not sit passively in the pews, waiting for the pastor to do all the work.

The apostle Paul tells us that pastors and teachers and other leaders in the church are not responsible to do all the work themselves, but "to equip his people for works of service, so that the body of Christ may be built up" (Ephesians 4:12). The pastors equip the people, and the people carry out the ministry of the church. Christians who have no ministry of their own are living stunted Christian lives. They are missing out on the excitement of following Jesus—and they are not fulfilling God's purpose for their lives. An anonymous poet once described the dilemma of those in the church who have no ministry of their own:

> The pastor is late,
>   He's forgotten the date.
> And what will the people do then,
>   Poor things!
> They'll sit in the pew,
>   With nothing to do,
> And sing a collection of hymns.
>   Poor things!

We need to make sure that doesn't describe our church.

Another principle that emerges from Nehemiah 3 is that believers should work together in unity and harmony. We should be one in the body of Christ. As you read through this chapter, you find that the phrase "next to" occurs twenty-one times. Zakkur son of Imri built next to the men of Jericho. Meshullam son of Berekiah made repairs next to Meremoth son of Uriah. And on and on, everyone working next to everyone else, encouraging each other, helping each other, living in harmony with each other.

The psalmist wrote, "How good and pleasant it is when God's people live together in unity!" (Psalm 133:1). Every person had his or her own job to do, but everyone worked in concert and in harmony with those on his left and on his right. The people worked together in unity.

Were there any shirkers among them? Were there some who failed to pull their share of the load? Yes, unfortunately, there were. And their names are noted in this account as well. Nehemiah writes, "The next section was repaired by the men of Tekoa, but their nobles would not put their shoulders to the work under their supervisors" (Nehemiah 3:5). God recorded in his Word both the heroes and the goof-offs. If you do not take up your ministry for the Lord, He will put your name down in the shirkers' column.

Fortunately, those who failed in their duties were few. Most worked hard and worked together. Nehemiah had so carefully and effectively organized the rebuilding effort that each person had a specific section of the wall or a gate assigned to him. Some workers exceeded all expectations and went above and beyond in the performance of their work. For example, Hanun and the residents of Zanoah repaired the Valley Gate, then went on to repair another five hundred yards of the wall (the length of five football fields!). After exceeding their own allotment of work, they didn't stop! They went on to help others with their work. And there are other individuals and groups mentioned who completed their own allotment, then assisted their friends and neighbors. Seven times in this chapter Nehemiah says that this or that individual or group "repaired another section" of the wall.

As a result of the extra effort on the part of some of the workers, a job that might have taken several months to finish was completed (as we shall later see) in just fifty-two days. This is an amazing accomplishment!

Another principle of cooperation emerges from Nehemiah 3: God has strategically placed us where He wants us, and we should serve Him eagerly wherever we are. Again and again in this passage, we see that many of these workers are making repairs within a few steps of their own front doors: "Jedaiah son of Harumaph made repairs opposite his house" (v. 10). "Benjamin and Hasshub made repairs in front of their house" (v. 23). And "Azariah son of Maaseiah, the son of Ananiah, made repairs beside his house" (v. 23), and so forth.

In verse 30, Nehemiah writes that "Meshullam son of Berekiah made repairs opposite his living quarters." The word translated living quarters literally means "chamber or apartment." This man may very well have been a bachelor, so he would not have had an actual house, but he repaired the wall closest to his bachelor's apartment.

This passage tells us a great deal about God's design for ministry. Where does God want you to conduct your ministry for Him? The answer is this: Wherever He has placed you, wherever you happen to be: your neighborhood, your office, your campus, your military unit, your home. Jesus once told His disciples, "You did not choose me, but I chose you and appointed you so that you might go and bear fruit—fruit that will last" (John 15:16). In the original language, the word translated appointed actually means "strategically placed." God has chosen and appointed you, and He strategically placed you where you are.

Here's another principle that emerges from this chapter: we must persevere until we get the job done. Everyone finished the work God gave them to do—except the so-called "nobles" of Tekoa, who didn't want to get dirt under their fingernails. Some had more work to do than others; some even finished their work early and went on to help their friends and neighbors. The ability to persevere is a mark of spiritual maturity. Mature believers always complete the work God has given them.

Proceed with Caution

As we explore Nehemiah 3, let's keep in mind the principle that the rebuilding of the wall and the restoration of its gates is an illuminating portrayal of the rebuilding of a broken life. You may be hurting right now because of choices you've made, habits you've developed, or sinful actions others have committed against you. The gates of your soul may lie in ruins, so that evil now has access to your spirit and your emotions. You are invaded frequently and upset quickly. This account reveals the areas you must rebuild in order to find deliverance and safety.

Each of the gates of Jerusalem can be seen to have a particular meaning and symbolic significance. As we look at the meaning of each gate, I want to acknowledge at the outset that some Bible teachers disapprove of the approach I'm about to take. They call this approach "allegorizing the Scriptures" or "spiritualizing the text." And they are correct in warning of the danger of making symbolic interpretations of Scripture. It's easy for the imagination to take over and assign arbitrary meanings that have no relation to the text. Instead of reading out of Scripture the meaning God has embedded there, we run the risk of reading into Scripture our own foolish human ideas.

Many cults and false doctrines have resulted from spiritualizing Scripture passages that should be read and understood in a purely literal way. Someone has well said, "He who spiritualizes God's Word lacks 'spiritual eyes' and tells 'spiritual lies.'" So we must approach the Bible with discernment and respect.

At the same time, our respect for God's Word requires that, whenever God speaks to us through pictures and symbols, we should be attentive to what He says to us. There is a legitimate way to approach the imagery and symbols of Scripture. The apostle Paul used allegory and symbols to interpret Old Testament passages, saying, "These things happened to them as examples and were written down as warnings for us, on whom the culmination of the ages has come" (1 Corinthians 10:11).

Whenever we interpret God's Word, we need to proceed with caution and with reverence for the truth God has placed there for us. If we observe the primary law of Bible interpretation—Scripture interprets Scripture—we can safely proceed through the account in Nehemiah 3, and we can apply these symbols to our lives today.

All of these symbols have been used elsewhere in Scripture, and they are used in a consistent way throughout the Bible. So those other passages of Scripture serve as guidelines for this interpretation of the symbols of Nehemiah 3.

The Sheep Gate, Fish Gate, and Jeshanah Gate

With these principles in mind, let's return to the first two verses of Nehemiah 3 and take a tour of the gates of Jerusalem, beginning with the first gate, the Sheep Gate:

> Eliashib the high priest and his fellow priests went to work and rebuilt the Sheep Gate. They dedicated it and set its doors in place, building as far as the Tower of the Hundred, which they dedicated, and as far as the Tower of Hananel. The men of Jericho built the adjoining section, and Zakkur son of Imri built next to them. (vv. 1–2)

The Sheep Gate was located where St. Stephen's Gate (sometimes called the Lion Gate) stands today. The Sheep Gate was at the northeast corner of the city. This gate was located where the sheep were kept for the temple sacrifices.

This gate can remind us of Isaiah's prophetic statement about Jesus the Messiah: "he was led like a lamb to the slaughter, and as a sheep before its shearers is silent, so he did not open his mouth" (Isaiah 53:7). Remember also that John the Baptist greeted Jesus with the words, "Look, the Lamb of God, who takes away the sin of the world!" (John 1:29). Sheep are a symbol of sacrifice in Scripture.

We can see the Sheep Gate as a symbol of the principle of the cross at work in the life of a follower of Christ. It is the place where you begin your life as a Christian. The Sheep Gate is the place where the old self, the natural self, is put to death. The old life passes away, replaced by the new life in Christ. As the apostle Paul told the believers in Corinth, "You are not your own; you were bought at a price" (1 Corinthians 6:19–20). The Sheep Gate can symbolize not only the sacrificial work of Christ on the cross but also the work of the cross in our lives.

When you came to Christ, you gave up control of your own life. You decided you would no longer do your own will. You were called to obey God and to do His will, following Him and walking with Him. Some of your old desires and natural urges had to be put to death. That is the principle of the cross and the principle of the Sheep Gate. Since we are crucified with Christ, we are dead to the world, and the world is dead to us. Selfishness and sinfulness must be sacrificed like a sheep on the temple altar. All of these principles of the Christian life are suggested by the symbol of the Sheep Gate, and that is why this gate comes first among all the gates of Jerusalem. It is vitally important that we keep the Sheep Gate of our lives in good repair as we grow in the Christian life.

Nehemiah's description of the rebuilding of the gates moves counterclockwise from the northeast corner of the city, along the wall of

Jerusalem, to the Fish Gate at the north-central point of the wall. Nehemiah writes:

> The Fish Gate was rebuilt by the sons of Hassenaah. They laid its beams and put its doors and bolts and bars in place. Meremoth son of Uriah, the son of Hakkoz, repaired the next section. Next to him Meshullam son of Berekiah, the son of Meshezabel, made repairs, and next to him Zadok son of Baana also made repairs. The next section was repaired by the men of Tekoa, but their nobles would not put their shoulders to the work under their supervisors. (Nehemiah 3:3–5)

The Fish Gate would have been located near the site of the present Damascus Gate. It is called the Fish Gate because the fishermen from Galilee and the coast brought their fish into the city through this gate. This gate can remind us of what the Lord said to His disciples: "Follow me, and I will make you fishers of men" (see Matthew 4:19 KJV). Fishing is a symbol of witnessing to others, of the importance of testifying before others that you belong to Christ. You witness by your words and actions.

A number of years ago, I was talking to a high school student who had gone to a secular camp for the summer. I asked him, "How did you get along as a Christian among nonbelievers?" He replied, "Oh, they never found out I was a Christian."

I was profoundly disappointed to hear that. This young man needed to repair the Fish Gate in his life. He needed to ask God to help him become more bold and fearless in his witness. God has called us to be fishers of men, casting our nets to draw souls to Him. I pray that you never have to stand before the Lord and say, "Oh, I never had to suffer persecution. I was never attacked or mocked for my faith. The world never found out I was a Christian."

Next we come to the Jeshanah Gate, which in Hebrew means "the Old Gate." It was located somewhere near the present Jaffa Gate. Nehemiah writes:

> The Jeshanah Gate was repaired by Joiada son of Paseah and Meshullam son of Besodeiah. They laid its beams and put its doors with their bolts and bars in place. Next to them, repairs were made by men from Gibeon and Mizpah—Melatiah of Gibeon and Jadon of Meronoth—places under the authority of the governor of Trans-Euphrates. Uzziel son of Harhaiah, one of the goldsmiths, repaired the next section; and Hananiah, one of the perfume-makers, made repairs next to that. They restored Jerusalem as far as the Broad Wall. Rephaiah son of Hur, ruler of a half-district of Jerusalem, repaired the next section. Adjoining this, Jedaiah son of Harumaph made repairs opposite his house, and Hattush son of Hashabneiah made repairs next to him. Malkijah son of Harim and Hasshub son of Pahath-Moab repaired another section and the Tower of the Ovens. (Nehemiah 3:6–11)

The Jeshanah Gate can be seen to represent the old ways of truth versus new illusions that lead to error. The world is constantly proposing something new—the New Age movement, Postmodernism, the New Left, Neo-Paganism, New Thought, Post-Protestantism, Post-Evangelicalism, and on and on. God's Word calls us back to the old way. As God told Israel through the prophet Jeremiah, "Stand at the crossroads and look; ask for the ancient paths, ask where the good way is, and walk in it, and you will find rest for your souls" (see Jeremiah 6:16).

Someone once said, "If something is new, it's not true; and if it's true, then it's now new." That is because truth remains the same throughout the centuries. Truth never changes. So the Old Gate, the Jeshanah Gate, can call us back to the time-tested paths of sound, ancient wisdom.

Many in the world today have departed from the great truths of Scripture. We are fallen creatures living under the authority of a sovereign God who can do what He wants. It's only by the grace of God that we can know Christ and be saved. These are old truths, and they are unchanging. New social movements, new religions, and new technologies wash over our society in wave after wave—yet human nature does not change, human sin does not change, and God's plan of salvation does not change. God is the same yesterday, today, and tomorrow, and we need to remember the old truths, symbolized by the Jeshanah Gate.

Gates of Humility, Elimination, and Cleansing

Our tour brings us next to the Valley Gate. Nehemiah writes: "The Valley Gate was repaired by Hanun and the residents of Zanoah. They rebuilt it and put its doors with their bolts and bars in place. They also repaired a thousand cubits of the wall as far as the Dung Gate" (Nehemiah 3:13).

The Valley Gate was located at the southwestern corner of Jerusalem. A valley in Scripture always represents humility and the judgment of pride in our lives. John Stott calls humility "that rarest and fairest of Christian virtues." If pride is the ultimate sin, then humility, its opposite, is the ultimate virtue. Peter tells us, "God opposes the proud but shows favor to the humble" (1 Peter 5:5).

I often remind myself of that verse when I'm tempted to be proud. I remember that if I act in pride, God will resist me. Do you want God working against you? I don't. When God resists someone, that person can expect total defeat. The resistance of God can never be overcome.

Not only does God resist the proud but He also shows favor to the humble. He gives grace to those who maintain a sense of humility. And humility means being willing to be instructed by God and to learn from Him. We do not have all the answers—but God does. We don't know how to handle the problems and crises that life throws at us—but God does. If we are proud, God will resist us; if we are humble, He will help us and give us grace.

The world applauds pride. The world rewards arrogance. But God rewards humility. This is the first lesson we must learn in the school of the Spirit. Jesus said, "Take my yoke upon you and learn from me, for I am gentle and humble in heart, and you will find rest for your souls," (Matthew 11:29). One reason so many people are restless today is that they have never learned to be gentle and humble in heart. Those who are genuinely humble find rest for their souls—and true peace of mind. All of this, it seems to me, is symbolized for us in the gate that represents humility, the Valley Gate.

Next we come to the Dung Gate. That's not a typo. That's the name of the gate. And like the other gates, the Dung Gate can be seen to have an important symbolic significance for our lives today. Nehemiah writes: "The Dung Gate was repaired by Malkijah son of Rekab, ruler of the district of Beth Hakkerem. He rebuilt it and put its doors with their bolts and bars in place" (Nehemiah 3:14).

The Dung Gate—it's not a pleasant name, but it is a necessary activity. It is the gate of elimination, the gate through which all the filth and rubbish and corruption passes out of the city and is taken to the garbage dump in the Hinnom Valley, outside Jerusalem.

Just as a city must eliminate its waste, we believers must eliminate the filth and corruption from our own lives. Paul urges us, "Dear friends, let us purify ourselves from everything that contaminates body and spirit, perfecting holiness out of reverence for God" (2 Corinthians 7:1). One reason many Christians fail to function as God intends is because they seldom use the Dung Gate. They do not eliminate moral and spiritual foulness, but they keep their sin and corruption inside.

Jesus said, "If your right eye causes you to stumble, gouge it out and throw it away. It is better for you to lose one part of your body than for your whole body to be thrown into hell. And if your right hand causes you to stumble, cut it off and throw it away. It is better for you to lose one part of your body than for your whole body to go into hell" (Matthew 5:29–30). It is actually better to lose an eye or a hand than to bottle up the filth and corruption within.

In spite of its ignoble name, the Dung Gate was vitally important to the health and well-being of the people of Jerusalem. In the same way, what the Dung Gate represents—the elimination of moral and spiritual corruption—is vitally important to the health and well-being of Christians today.

The Dung Gate was the southernmost gate of the city. Continuing counterclockwise around the city, the wall makes a sharp northeastward turn. The next gate we reach is the sixth gate, the Fountain Gate:

> The Fountain Gate was repaired by Shallun son of Kol-Hozeh, ruler of the district of Mizpah. He rebuilt it, roofing it over and putting its doors and bolts and bars in place. He also repaired the wall of the Pool of Siloam, by the King's Garden, as far as the steps going down from the City of David. Beyond him, Nehemiah son of Azbuk, ruler of a half-district of Beth Zur, made repairs up to a point opposite the tombs of David, as far as the artificial pool and the House of the Heroes. (Nehemiah 3:15–16)

The Fountain Gate was at the end of the Pool of Siloam, low in the valley in the south. This gate speaks, of course, of a fountain springing up. It can reminds us of Jesus's words in John 7 where he spoke of "rivers of living water" (John 7:38) flowing from our lives. This can be seen as a picture of the ministry of the Holy Spirit, welling up in our lives like a bubbling spring and overflowing into the lives of the people around us.

In Ephesians 5:18, the apostle Paul tells us not to be drunk on wine but to be filled with the Holy Spirit—and in the original language, Paul actually tells us to keep being filled with the Spirit. The filling of the Spirit is a continual, ongoing process of filling, cleansing, and overflowing. The Spirit is a continuous fountain in our lives.

Notice that the Fountain Gate comes immediately after the Dung Gate in this account. After the foulness and corruption is removed from our lives via the Dung Gate, any remnants of uncleanness are cleansed away by the overflowing fountain of the Spirit, who washes us clean day by day. But the Spirit can only work in our lives by our consent. We must keep the Fountain Gate in good repair so the fountain of the Spirit can flow freely in our lives.

The Gate That Did Not Need Repairs

Next, Nehemiah describes a series of repairs that were made in various sections of the wall between the Fountain Gate and the next gate to the north, the Water Gate:

> Next to him, the repairs were made by the Levites under Rehum son of Bani. Beside him, Hashabiah, ruler of half the district of Keilah, carried out repairs for his district. Next to him, the repairs were made by their fellow Levites under Binnui son of Henadad, ruler of the other half-district of Keilah. Next to him, Ezer son of Jeshua, ruler of Mizpah, repaired another section, from a point facing the ascent to the armory as far as the angle of the wall. Next to him, Baruch son of Zabbai zealously repaired another section, from the angle to the entrance of the house of Eliashib the high priest. Next to him, Meremoth son of Uriah, the son of Hakkoz, repaired another section, from the entrance of Eliashib's house to the end of it.

The repairs next to him were made by the priests from the surrounding region. Beyond them, Benjamin and Hasshub made repairs in front of their house; and next to them, Azariah son of Maaseiah, the son of Ananiah, made repairs beside his house. Next to him, Binnui son of Henadad repaired another section, from Azariah's house to the angle and the corner, and Palal son of Uzai worked opposite the angle and the tower projecting from the upper palace near the court of the guard. Next to him, Pedaiah son of Parosh and the temple servants living on the hill of Ophel made repairs up to a point opposite the Water Gate toward the east and the projecting tower. Next to them, the men of Tekoa repaired another section, from the great projecting tower to the wall of Ophel. (Nehemiah 3:17–27)

The Water Gate was located at the spring of Gihon, where Hezekiah's tunnel begins. The Scriptures record that King Hezekiah "blocked the upper outlet of the Gihon spring and channeled the water down to the west side of the City of David. He succeeded in everything he undertook" (see 2 Chronicles 32:30). Today, you can walk through Hezekiah's tunnel, which is longer than five football fields and was cut by hand through the rock to carry water to the Pool of Siloam, an astounding feat of engineering accomplished eight centuries before Christ.

In the Bible, water is a symbol for the Word of God. The Water Gate reminds us of our continual need for refreshment from the Word of God. It's important to notice in this account that no one made any repairs to the Water Gate. No repairs were needed.

God's Word never needs improvement or repair. The Word of God is indestructible. It lasts forever. In order to experience refreshment from God's Word, we need to rediscover and re-inhabit it. Do you need to re-inhabit the "Water Gate" of God's Word? If so, you need to read and study the Bible.

Jesus, in his reply to Satan the tempter in the wilderness, said, "It is written: 'Man shall not live on bread alone, but on every word that comes from the mouth of God'" (Matthew 4:4; see also Luke 4:4). If you want your life filled with the joy God intended for you, then drink deeply from the Word of God.

The Horse Gate—the Gate of Battle

Next in our tour of the gates of Jerusalem, we come to the Horse Gate. Nehemiah writes: "Above the Horse Gate, the priests made repairs, each in front of his own house. Next to them, Zadok son of Immer made repairs opposite his house" (Nehemiah 3:28–29).

From the Water Gate to the Horse Gate there is a long stretch of unbroken wall. The Horse Gate is in the northern section of the east wall of the city. In the Scriptures, horses are always a symbol of war. The Horse Gate reminds us that the Christian life is not a Sunday school picnic. We live out our lives on a battlefield, and throughout our lives, we will be relentlessly attacked. Sometimes the enemy of our souls places a long, merciless siege on our lives, an attack that seems to go on and on forever. At other times, our enemy launches a sudden surprise attack.

In the midst of the spiritual warfare that is an ever-present fact of the Christian life, there is great joy in our lives. This life is not without struggle, but Jesus, our commander, is greater than our foe. He will win the battle. The words of the Isaac Watts's hymn "Am I a Soldier of the Cross?" offer a great perspective on our spiritual battles:

> Am I a soldier of the Cross—
>   A follower of the Lamb?
> And shall I fear to own His cause,
>   Or blush to speak His name?

In the name, the precious name,
  Of Him who died for me,
Through grace I'll win the promised crown,
  Whate'er my cross may be.

Must I be carried to the skies
  On flowery beds of ease,
While others fought to win the prize
  And sailed through bloody seas?

Are there no foes for me to face?
  Must I not stem the flood?
Is this vile world a friend to grace,
  To help me on to God?

Since I must fight if I would reign,
  Increase my courage, Lord!
I'll bear the toil, endure the pain,
  Supported by Thy Word.[2]

Those are empowering words from a great hymn of the faith, and they remind us of the battles that are symbolically represented by the Horse Gate.

Gates of Hope and Expectation— and Judgment and Reward

Next, we come to the ninth gate, the East Gate, which is today known as the Golden Gate. Nehemiah writes:

Next to him, Shemaiah son of Shekaniah, the guard at the East Gate, made repairs. Next to him, Hananiah son of Shelemiah, and Hanun, the sixth son of Zalaph, repaired another section. Next to them, Meshullam son of Berekiah made repairs opposite his living quarters. (Nehemiah 3:29–30)

The East Gate is a short distance from the Horse Gate on the northern side of the eastern wall. It stands opposite the temple area and faces the rising sun. Thus it can speak to us of hope and expectation. It is the gate through which the Messiah will enter the city of Jerusalem when He returns.

The East Gate—the gate of the hope and expectation of the Lord's Second Coming—is a gate that is often in ruins in the lives of Christians. People must have hope in order to go on living. Again and again down through history some people who have given up hope have made the tragic decision to end their lives. In fact, I once read the story of a mother who, through some combination of hopeless circumstances and mental illness, chose to take the lives of her two little children as well as her own because she didn't want them to live in a world of (as she saw it) hopelessness and despair.

The symbol of the East Gate can remind us that God has a glorious hope awaiting all those who place their trust in Him. Even though the life of Jesus the Messiah appeared to end in despair and tragedy, Jesus told His disciples that He would rise again. He also told His disciples that He would come again to receive them and take them to heaven: "When these things begin to take place, stand up and lift up your heads, because your redemption is drawing near" (Luke 21:28).

Because Jesus has left us this unconquerable hope, we must not despair, even in the midst of our trials and sorrows. Because of the hope within us, we believers ought to be like teakettles that sing the loudest when they are up to their necks in hot water.

Finally, Nehemiah takes us to the last gate, which is called the Inspection Gate.

> Next to him, Malkijah, one of the goldsmiths, made repairs as far as the house of the temple servants and the merchants, opposite the Inspection Gate, and as far as the room above the corner; and

between the room above the corner and the Sheep Gate the gold-smiths and merchants made repairs. (Nehemiah 3:31–32)

In the original Hebrew, the term translated here as *Inspection Gate* literally means "the appointed place." The book of Hebrews tells us, "It is appointed unto men once to die, but after this the judgment" (Hebrews 9:27 KJV). In other words, when we reach the appointed place and our lives are over, it is time for the Inspection.

We can see the Inspection Gate as a reminder that we must all give an account to God for our life's journey. We must learn at last the truth about our lives as God sees us. We will see the entire span of our lives, from birth to death, exactly as it occurred. We will see ourselves doing and saying things that, right now, we can't even recall.

Will the Lord affirm us for the things we have done and said? Or will we review the account of our lives with remorse and regret?

Please understand. The Scriptures encourage us with the assurance that there is now no condemnation for those who are in Christ Jesus (see Romans 8:1). And Paul also tells us that we who labor for the Lord and carry out His commands in obedience "shall receive his own reward according to his own labor" (see 1 Corinthians 3:8 KJV). For the faithful believer, the Inspection Gate is a place of joy and rewards. But for many, the Inspection Gate is an appointment with everlasting regret.

The final verse of this text brings us full circle, back to the Sheep Gate, where we began. As we saw earlier, the Sheep Gate can represent the cross, and the cross must be at the beginning and end of our journey through this life. The Sheep Gate, located near the altar of sacrifice, reminds us that out of death comes life. Out of the subjection of our natural desires to the will of God comes the life of God, filling our lives with blessing.

As a young boy, not even in my teens, I learned a hymn that has stayed with me throughout my life. We don't hear it sung very much these days, yet the words are meaningful, comforting, and encouraging. It's called "The Way of the Cross Leads Home."[3]

> I must needs go home by the way of the cross,
>   There's no other way but this;
> I shall ne'er get sight of the Gates of Light,
>   If the way of the cross I miss.
>
> I must needs go on in the blood-sprinkled way,
>   The path that the Savior trod,
> If I ever climb to the heights sublime,
>   Where the soul is at home with God.
>
> *Refrain:*
>
> The way of the cross leads home,
>   The way of the cross leads home,
> It is sweet to know as I onward go,
>   The way of the cross leads home.

This is a beautiful expression of the teaching in Nehemiah 3. As we make our way around the walls of Jerusalem, each gate reminds us and instructs us about an aspect of the Christian life. We need to be reminded. We need to be watchful. We need to remember these truths as we rebuild and repair the walls of our lives. Only as we repair these gates can we become all that God intended us to be.

5

†††††††††††††††

DON'T BACK DOWN—
BUILD UP!

Nehemiah 4 and 5

We have all heard of Murphy's Law—the principle commonly expressed as, "If anything can go wrong, it will." There are countless corollaries of Murphy's Law. For example, it is said that if you try to fix something, Murphy's Law dictates that it will take longer than predicted, cost more than expected, and break down before it is paid for.

Although Murphy's Law is well known, few people know where Murphy's Law came from or that it was actually named for a real person, Air Force Captain Ed Murphy. He was an engineer on rocket sled tests in the late 1940s when the Air Force was trying to determine how much stress a pilot could withstand. Captain Murphy was in charge of "strain gauges" and other sensors used to measure physical stress on the pilot.

On one occasion, Captain Murphy and his assistant installed the sensors for a rocket sled test. The test pilot was strapped into the rocket sled, the sensors were attached, the jets were fired, and the rocket sled shot down the track. The test went smoothly—but when the engineers checked the readings, they noticed that the gauges had failed to record any data from the test. Captain Murphy immediately blamed the technician who had assisted him, saying, "If there's any way to do it wrong, he will." Those who heard Captain Murphy later reworded his complaint into the famous adage, "If anything can go wrong, it will."

That was the origin of Murphy's Law.

Yet the basic principles of Murphy's Law existed centuries before Captain Ed Murphy was born. As we come to Nehemiah 4, we see that Nehemiah has made every attempt to account for possible problems and setbacks with the reconstruction effort. He has prayed. He has planned. He has carefully assessed the project. He has involved the entire population of greater Jerusalem in the effort to rebuild the walls.

But Nehemiah underestimated the power of Murphy's Law. Something is about to go wrong that he didn't foresee. In Nehemiah 4, Nehemiah comes face-to-face with severe and violent opposition to his plan for rebuilding the walls of Jerusalem.

As we've seen, the rebuilding of the walls is a picture of the steps to recovery from emotional wounds and spiritual brokenness in our own lives. We have witnessed Nehemiah's anguish over the ruined state of Jerusalem, the political and spiritual capital of his nation. Nehemiah's heartbreak echoes the anguish we feel when our own lives have been broken by sinful habits, destructive attitudes, and feelings of bitterness or resentment.

We also saw Nehemiah seize without doubt or hesitation the opportunity to rebuild. When opportunities for healing and recovery come to us, we must not hold back in reluctance or fear. If the gospel is explained to you and you feel God's Spirit tugging at your heart, don't say, "I have plenty of time to make a decision for Christ." Now is the time. Don't hesitate. Seize the opportunity. If you feel God prompting you to join a Bible study or recovery group, seek counseling, or confide in a trusted Christian friend, now is the time.

Nehemiah honestly assessed the magnitude of the challenge before him. He didn't examine the situation through rose-colored glasses. He didn't kid himself and say, "This will be easy." Instead, he faced the situation squarely, and he gave the people a message similar to the one Winston Churchill gave the people of Great Britain at the outbreak of World War II: "I have nothing to offer but blood, toil, tears, and sweat."

Nehemiah didn't realize the full extent of blood, toil, tears, and sweat that lay before him. He didn't realize how intense the opposition would be. Murphy's Law swings into action, and the real battle begins.

The Weapon of Ridicule

Like Nehemiah, you and I have an enemy who opposes us with vicious hate, craftiness, and power. Martin Luther described our enemy in "A Mighty Fortress Is Our God."

> For still our ancient foe
> doth seek to work us woe;
> His craft and power are great,
> and, armed with cruel hate,
> On earth is not his equal.[1]

No earthly power is the equal of this ancient foe. Whenever we attempt to recover from the hurts of the past, we will suffer opposition. Just when it seems that we are on the road to recovery, whatever can go wrong will go wrong. Our enemy may oppose us as we make our way through natural circumstances—illness, accident, a financial calamity, the loss of someone close to us, a natural disaster. Or our enemy may oppose us through other people—a friend who turns on us, an unreasonable neighbor, an angry boss, a gossipy coworker, a rebellious child, an unfaithful spouse.

The attacks of the enemy can come at any moment, from any direction, when we least expect it. In Nehemiah's case, the attack came through the ridicule and threats of three men who sought to discourage the workers and halt the rebuilding. Nehemiah records:

> When Sanballat heard that we were rebuilding the wall, he became angry and was greatly incensed. He ridiculed the Jews, and in the presence of his associates and the army of Samaria, he said, "What are those feeble Jews doing? Will they restore their wall? Will they offer sacrifices? Will they finish in a day? Can they bring the stones back to life from those heaps of rubble—burned as they are?"
>
> Tobiah the Ammonite, who was at his side, said, "What they are building—even a fox climbing up on it would break down their wall of stones!" (Nehemiah 4:1–3)

This is a common and potent form of attack that is often more devastating than we realize. We like to think that we have physical courage and that we would be willing to risk our lives for God and for other people—yet we often find ourselves intimidated and deterred from doing God's will out of fear of people laughing at us, mocking us, or attacking our reputations.

Our enemy is not creative. He inspires people to use the same verbal ploys again and again: "You're just going through a 'religious' phase—do you think you're better than us?" "So you've 'got religion'—how long do you think that will last?" How many times has Satan inspired worldly people to say such things? Why should Satan change his tactics if the same old approach still works?

I once knew a man who told me that his alcoholism was destroying his health and ruining his relationships with his wife and children. He knew he should seek help to stop drinking. Yet he wouldn't take the steps to save his life and save his family. Why? Because he had friends—drinking buddies—who would mock him and ridicule him if he ever stopped drinking. So, to avoid being mocked and laughed at, he kept drinking. He ultimately destroyed his life.

Today, countless people are hooked on drugs—either street drugs or prescription drugs that are sold illegally on the street. They feel trapped, and they know their lives are being destroyed. Yet they fear the ridicule and peer pressure they would face if they were to walk away from the drug culture.

Ridicule is a powerful weapon of our enemy, Satan, as he seeks to neutralize us and destroy us. Why do we care what other people think? Why do we care what our enemies think? Why do we care what our so-called "friends" think as they try to keep us trapped in self-destructive behavior? We should only care what God thinks of us. Let our enemies ridicule us all they want. God's opinion is the only one that matters.

It's fascinating to keep Nehemiah 4 open as we watch the daily news from the Middle East. It's amazing that, after all those centuries, so little has changed in that region of the world. The enemies of Israel in those days are still Israel's enemies today. Sanballat was the governor of Samaria, which is the region of Palestine we now call "the West Bank." Tobiah was the representative of a country that was then known as Ammon, now called Jordan. Later, in verse 7, we will read about the opposition of "the Arabs, the Ammonites and the people of Ashdod." Where is Ashdod today? It is the Gaza Strip, a small and troubled Palestinian territory that borders Egypt,

Israel, and the Mediterranean Sea. It's a densely populated land predominantly made up of Sunni Muslims, with Hamas and other militant groups continually engaged in hostilities against Israel. In the Middle East, what's old is always new again.

One of the tactics employed by the enemies of Israel to this day, along with all the mortar shells and Katyusha rockets, is mocking and ridicule. After one attempt by Israel to suppress Palestinian rocket attacks from Gaza, the leader of a terrorist organization boasted, "The Israelis' first goal was to destroy Palestinian leadership—they failed. Their second goal was to destroy our missile systems—they failed. Their third goal was to make themselves appear strong and invulnerable to attack—they actually made themselves weaker."

These taunts sound little different from the taunts of Sanballat and Tobiah: "What are those feeble Jews doing? Will they restore their wall?" And, "What they are building—even a fox climbing up on it would break down their wall of stones!"

How do we respond to the taunts of our opponents? It might be easier to understand the mockery of our earthly enemies when we realize that, in many cases, the real source of the persecution we face is our spiritual enemy. And spiritual opposition requires a spiritual response.

That is what we see in the life of Nehemiah—a spiritual response to the mockery and scorn of his enemies. Nehemiah's first impulse, when he is attacked and mocked by these enemies, is to go to his knees in prayer. Nehemiah prays:

> Hear us, our God, for we are despised. Turn their insults back on their own heads. Give them over as plunder in a land of captivity. Do not cover up their guilt or blot out their sins from your sight, for they have thrown insults in the face of the builders. (vv. 4–5)

The margin note in the New International Version offers an alternative translation of the last sentence: "Do not cover up their guilt or blot out their sins from your sight, for they have aroused your anger before the face of the builders." In other words, Nehemiah is saying that this attack is an insult not only against the builders but also against God himself. Nehemiah does not bother arguing with his opponents or retaliating against them. He does not insult them back. He says that this is an insult against God, and he leaves the matter in the lap of heaven, trusting God to administer justice against the enemies of Israel.

Nehemiah's response reminds us of Peter's description of Jesus at the crucifixion: "When they hurled their insults at him, he did not retaliate; when he suffered, he made no threats" (1 Peter 2:23). This is a helpful picture of how we should handle these kinds of insults and attacks.

Even though Nehemiah's response is similar to that of the Lord Jesus, in that he does not retaliate against his enemies, Nehemiah's prayer is not the kind of prayer Jesus prayed on the cross. Jesus said, "Father, forgive them, for they do not know what they are doing" (Luke 23:34). And Jesus taught us to bless those who persecute us and to pray for our enemies.

How, then, do we square Nehemiah's prayer with the teachings of our Lord? The answer, of course, is to remember who is praying. This is not Nehemiah, the ordinary believer, who has been injured by the personal insults of a fellow citizen. Nehemiah is praying in his official capacity as the governor of Judah. He is praying about the need to maintain order and peace in the land. He is praying as a man in official authority who is seeking to solve a problem of persistent human evil.

A number of years ago in a California community not far from my home, an emotionally disturbed drifter stood outside an elementary school playground while children played at recess. He raised a semi-automatic weapon and opened fire, killing five schoolchildren and wounding thirty-one other children and a teacher. Then he committed suicide.

Suppose he had lived, was captured, and stood trial for the massacre. How should the governing authorities treat this man? Should the prosecutor, the judge, and the jury all say, "We forgive this man, for he didn't know what he was doing"? Should the authorities dispense mercy to this killer?

Absolutely not. The first task of government is not mercy but justice. If the families of the children who were killed or wounded could say to this man, "We forgive you," or if one of the wounded children can say, "I forgive you," that would be an act of Christlike forgiveness. But if the government were to say to a cold-blooded killer, "The people of this state forgive you. Society forgives you. Go in peace," that would not be Christlike mercy and forgiveness—that would be a horrifying travesty of justice. The blood of those children would cry out for justice.

So as Nehemiah prayed for these opponents of Israel, he didn't pray that God would have mercy on them. He did not pray as an individual who had been personally insulted. He prayed as the governor of the province of Judah. And that is why he prayed, "Turn their insults back on their own heads. Give them over as plunder in a land of captivity. Do not cover up their guilt or blot out their sins from your sight, for they have aroused your anger before the face of the builders."

This prayer was Governor Nehemiah's plea for justice.

The Sword and the Trowel

Having prayed, Nehemiah returned to the work of rebuilding. He refused to allow opposition to destroy his confidence or slow him down. "So we rebuilt the wall till all of it reached half its height, for the people worked with all their heart" (Nehemiah 4:6).

So the work continued—but the enemies of God weren't giving up. They grew even angrier, and resolved to use violence:

> But when Sanballat, Tobiah, the Arabs, the Ammonites and the people of Ashdod heard that the repairs to Jerusalem's walls had gone ahead and that the gaps were being closed, they were very angry. They all plotted together to come and fight against Jerusalem and stir up trouble against it. But we prayed to our God and posted a guard day and night to meet this threat (vv. 7–9).

The enemy mobilized and escalated the attack, plotting violent action. When you become effective for God, the enemies of God will try to put you out of business. They will start with words—but they often escalate to violence.

Once again, we see that Nehemiah responded both spiritually and pragmatically. He led the community in prayer to God—and he posted a twenty-four-hour guard to meet the threat posed by these enemies. Nehemiah was a role model of prayer—and preparedness. His perfect balance of a spiritual response with a practical response is a picture of how we, as believers, should face threats and opposition that come our way.

Still, the enemy persisted and went on to launch a propaganda campaign: "Meanwhile, the people in Judah said, 'The strength of the laborers is giving out, and there is so much rubble that we cannot rebuild the wall'" (v. 10).

This is understandable. There was an enormous amount of debris to be cleared away before they could even reach the walls. It must have been a discouraging challenge. My wife and I once moved out of a house where we had lived for thirty-three years, and the amount of stuff we had to clear away was often disheartening. We thought the task would never end. So the people of Jerusalem had reached a point of exhaustion and frustration.

The enemy saw their discouragement and took advantage of the people at their emotional low point:

> Also our enemies said, "Before they know it or see us, we will be right there among them and will kill them and put an end to the work."
> Then the Jews who lived near them came and told us ten times over, "Wherever you turn, they will attack us." (vv. 11–12)

When you begin to right wrongs, wrongdoers will try to stop you. Blow the whistle on an immoral or illegal practice at work, and you can expect to be demoted or fired. Try to shut down a drug dealer or pornographer in your neighborhood, and you'll be threatened—or worse. Nehemiah and the people of Jerusalem were trying to rebuild the broken walls and burned gates of the city—and their opponents plotted death and destruction.

Notice how frightened many of the people of Jerusalem were. They went to Nehemiah not once or twice, but ten times and warned Nehemiah that their enemies were plotting an attack. It's important to understand Nehemiah's response to this threat, because this is how you and I should respond in similar situations.

First, Nehemiah carefully assessed the situation. "Therefore I stationed some of the people behind the lowest points of the wall at the exposed places, posting them by families, with their swords, spears and bows. After I looked things over . . ." (vv. 13–14).

From what we know of Nehemiah, it appears that he never rushed into a situation. Instead, he carefully examined every angle and evaluated what he needed to do to achieve success. He always began by gathering the facts. We need to emulate this approach and find out exactly where we face our most dangerous attacks.

Are we under attack in our habits and addictions? Are we under attack in our attitudes and thinking? Are we under attack in our bitter and resentful emotions? Are we under attack in our lusts and greed? Are we under attack from within or without? We need to identify where the enemy is attacking us—and we must post a guard at that point. That's how Nehemiah dealt with this threat.

Following the attack on Pearl Harbor on December 7, 1941, a popular song was released to boost the morale of Americans at home and abroad. This song is said to have been based on a real quote and a real incident during the Pearl Harbor attack. In the song, which is a bit different from the actual incident from which it was taken, a military chaplain is leading a group of sailors in Sunday morning worship when the enemy attacks from the sky. The sailors leap to their posts and the battle is on.

In the song, the chaplain sees a machine-gunner get hit by enemy fire. Then the gunner's mate is also hit. So the chaplain puts his Bible down, leaps into the gun turret, and begins returning fire. As he blasts away at the enemy planes, the chaplain shouts to his fellows, "Praise the Lord and pass the ammunition!"

That is what's happening here in Nehemiah 4. The people are building, they are praising God, and they are also prepared for battle. They are ready to defend the work God has called them to do.

Second, Nehemiah reviews the spiritual resources available to them.

> After I looked things over, I stood up and said to the nobles, the officials and the rest of the people, "Don't be afraid of them. Remember the Lord, who is great and awesome, and fight for your families, your sons and your daughters, your wives and your homes."
>
> When our enemies heard that we were aware of their plot and that God had frustrated it, we all returned to the wall, each to our own work. (vv. 14–15)

As believers in God, Nehemiah and the people of Jerusalem had a power in their lives that their enemies knew nothing about.

They had invisible resources for times of danger. Their great and awesome God would stand with them in the crisis. Remembering that God was with them, they experienced a resurgence of courage. It was the enemy, not the people of Jerusalem, who ended up being intimidated and frustrated. God's people continued to build, confident that God himself would fight for them.

One of my favorite New Testament passages is in Paul's second letter to Timothy. There Paul, a prisoner in Rome, writes to Timothy, a rather timid young man who is all alone, ministering in the city of Ephesus. Timothy felt discouraged because of the enormity of the challenge of being a pastor and evangelist in that pagan city. So Paul gave Timothy this word of advice: "Remember Jesus Christ, raised from the dead, descended from David. This is my gospel" (2 Timothy 2:8).

Paul wanted Timothy to remember that Jesus is risen and that he was raised from the dead by the awesome power of God. This same God was with Timothy in all of his trials, in spite of all opposition. He wanted Timothy to remember that by God's power he could stand against the worst temptations and threats that might come against him.

Nehemiah goes on to describe his readiness for the coming threats and opposition:

From that day on, half of my men did the work, while the other half were equipped with spears, shields, bows and armor. The officers posted themselves behind all the people of Judah who were building the wall. Those who carried materials did their work with one hand and held a weapon in the other, and each of the builders wore his sword at his side as he worked. But the man who sounded the trumpet stayed with me. (Nehemiah 4:16–18)

The people of Jerusalem had to combine work with war. Each man had to carry his trowel in one hand and his sword in the other.

It didn't matter if opposition came or not—each man was ready to get the job done. The job might be building the wall—or the job might be repelling a murderous invader. Each worker was fully prepared for either task.

Charles Haddon Spurgeon was a great English preacher during the nineteenth century. He published a newspaper in his church called *The Sword and the Trowel*—a name clearly derived from Nehemiah 4. Spurgeon said that Christians should always be building the kingdom of God—yet they should also be ready for battle at any moment.

Next, Nehemiah illustrates for us a principle of blended faith and preparation:

> Then I said to the nobles, the officials and the rest of the people, "The work is extensive and spread out, and we are widely separated from each other along the wall. Wherever you hear the sound of the trumpet, join us there. Our God will fight for us!" (vv. 19–20)

Nehemiah wanted the people to know that God would fight for them—but he also wanted them to know that they had to be prepared to serve as God's instruments in that fight. The work of rebuilding would cause them to be spread out and separated from one another—but at the sound of the trumpet, they all had to gather wherever the battle might be.

Both the rebuilding and the preparation for battle required a great deal of self-sacrifice. Many would have to work through the day then serve an extra watch as guards by night. They would sacrifice sleep and time with their families until the job was completed. Nehemiah concludes:

> So we continued the work with half the men holding spears, from the first light of dawn till the stars came out. At that time I also said

to the people, "Have every man and his helper stay inside Jerusalem at night, so they can serve us as guards by night and as workers by day." Neither I nor my brothers nor my men nor the guards with me took off our clothes; each had his weapon, even when he went for water. (vv. 21–23)

In wartime, even a good night's sleep is a luxury. The people of Jerusalem were on guard day and night, alert and vigilant. They sacrificed their comfort for the rebuilding effort—and the war effort. Like the apostle Paul, they were ready to endure hardship for the sake of the Lord.

An End to Oppression

In Nehemiah 5, their enemy—their real, unseen enemy, Satan himself—tries another approach. Nehemiah has successfully thwarted the threat of attack from without. Now he faces a problem from within his own ranks: "Now the men and their wives raised a great outcry against their fellow Jews" (v. 1).

The people should be celebrating victory over their foes. Instead, there is internal strife, neighbor against neighbor. In your struggle to rebuild some broken area of your life, you may run into problems and opposition from the people closest to you—your family members, your neighbors, your brothers and sisters in the Lord. Here in Nehemiah 5, the clash is between the workers and the officials, between the laborers and the overseers working on the project. It is, in fact, a class struggle between the privileged class and the working class. Nehemiah explains: "Some were saying, 'We and our sons and daughters are numerous; in order for us to eat and stay alive, we must get grain'" (v. 2).

Because the people were spending so much time working on the walls day and night, they had no time to plant crops and make a living. Yet they had to eat. In fact, they were going into debt to rebuild the walls—and they were putting their families at risk: "Others were saying, 'We are mortgaging our fields, our vineyards and our homes to get grain during the famine'" (v. 3).

Have you ever had to mortgage your property to make a living? Have you ever been forced to borrow against your home or your life insurance merely to keep your family from going hungry? This was the complaint many people made to Nehemiah. And there were worse complaints:

> Still others were saying, "We have had to borrow money to pay the king's tax on our fields and vineyards. Although we are of the same flesh and blood as our fellow Jews and though our children are as good as theirs, yet we have to subject our sons and daughters to slavery. Some of our daughters have already been enslaved, but we are powerless, because our fields and our vineyards belong to others." (vv. 4–5)

If you've ever had trouble paying your taxes, you know that the IRS will give you the option of putting your tax bill on a credit card. That is essentially what many people in Jerusalem were required to do, even as they were volunteering to rebuild the walls of the city. Though they were donating their time to rebuild the walls, they are unable to pay their taxes and their debts—and they were subjecting their wives and children to the humiliating risk of being enslaved. Some of their daughters had already been forced into slavery.

These were justified complaints. Nehemiah listened—and he became angry with the oppressors of the people. So he took action:

> When I heard their outcry and these charges, I was very angry. I pondered them in my mind and then accused the nobles and officials. I told them, "You are charging your own people interest!" So I called together a large meeting to deal with them and said:

"As far as possible, we have bought back our fellow Jews who were sold to the Gentiles. Now you are selling your own people, only for them to be sold back to us!" They kept quiet, because they could find nothing to say.

So I continued, "What you are doing is not right. Shouldn't you walk in the fear of our God to avoid the reproach of our Gentile enemies? I and my brothers and my men are also lending the people money and grain. But let us stop charging interest! Give back to them immediately their fields, vineyards, olive groves and houses, and also the interest you are charging them—one percent of the money, grain, new wine and olive oil." (vv. 6–8)

Lending money at interest is a common practice today. The Jewish people were allowed to charge interest on money lent to non-Jews—but charging interest on loans to fellow Jews was prohibited. Moses had said that when a Jew lent money to another Jew, he was not to charge any interest. He was to lend the money as if he were lending to his very own brother.

How much interest were these Jewish lenders charging their fellow Jews? One percent per month, or twelve percent per year. This does not sound excessive to us, but it was an outrageous interest rate in Nehemiah's time. I wonder what Nehemiah would have thought of credit card interest rates today.

The lenders who charged high interest rates were ashamed, and they repented. They not only agreed to end this practice of usury but they also promised to return the profits they had already made from the practice: "We will give it back," they said. "And we will not demand anything more from them. We will do as you say" (v. 12).

The people who had engaged in usury were stricken in their conscience because they knew that the Scriptures condemned what they had done. For years, they had rationalized their exploitation of their Jewish brothers and sisters, and they had excused themselves.

But now they had no excuse. So they promised to stop the practice and to give back what they had taken in the past.

As believers, we need to be very careful about maintaining Christian integrity and ethical standards, especially in how we relate to fellow Christians. We must always conduct our business dealings fairly and never take advantage of other people. There is nothing wrong with making a profit and providing for our families, but we should never oppress or exploit others to make ourselves rich.

Nehemiah was encouraged by the promise these people made to stop exploiting their fellow Jews, but he wanted them to go beyond a mere promise:

> Then I summoned the priests and made the nobles and officials take an oath to do what they had promised. I also shook out the folds of my robe and said, "In this way may God shake out of their house and possessions anyone who does not keep this promise. So may such a person be shaken out and emptied!"
>
> At this the whole assembly said, "Amen," and praised the LORD. And the people did as they had promised. (vv. 12–13)

When Nehemiah shook the folds of his garment as a visible expression of how God would shake the life and the household of anyone who violated his oath, he was using a common ancient Middle Eastern custom of emphasizing the seriousness of the matter. He wanted the people to understand that God took the matter very seriously and would hold them to their oath.

Nehemiah's Honest Government

Nehemiah 5 deals with Nehemiah's actions to quell internal strife in the Jewish community. He first uncovered the real cause of that strife, and he showed that the core problem was human greed—people exploiting their neighbors for profit. He confronted this sin, which the wealthy overseers of the community committed against their poorer brothers and sisters in the Jewish community. Nehemiah rebuked them and showed them it was wrong. Then he had them promise, by God's help, to end this practice and repay what they had taken.

As a leader, Nehemiah understood that it is sometimes necessary to state the painful truth and confront wrongdoing so justice and healing can begin. Most of us shy away from confrontation, but when God calls us to confront sin, it is cowardly to keep silent. Nehemiah was no coward. He boldly confronted that sin.

Next, Nehemiah contrasts his tenure as governor of the land of Judah against the tenure of his predecessors:

> Moreover, from the twentieth year of King Artaxerxes, when I was appointed to be their governor in the land of Judah, until his thirty-second year—twelve years—neither I nor my brothers ate the food allotted to the governor. But the earlier governors—those preceding me—placed a heavy burden on the people and took forty shekels of silver from them in addition to food and wine. Their assistants also lorded it over the people. But out of reverence for God I did not act like that. Instead, I devoted myself to the work on this wall. All my men were assembled there for the work; we did not acquire any land. (vv. 14–16)

This is a familiar picture. Ever since government was instituted, governmental officials have enriched themselves by exploiting their power over the people. Those who flatter themselves by calling themselves "public servants" frequently serve only themselves, enhancing their lavish lifestyles while treating their constituents with contempt.

People today are becoming increasingly aware of the astounding level of corruption in their government. According to *Forbes* magazine, the wealthiest counties in America tend to cluster around Washington, D.C. Why? Because that's where the "government industrial complex" is located. Taxpayer money flows like water into the Beltway, and it is sometimes distributed in exchange for political favors. Middle-class people enter politics, serve a few terms, then retire as multimillionaires.

This is not to say that all politicians are corrupt. Far from it. But corruption is rampant in government today and always has been. This is no excuse for being disobedient or disrespectful to our leaders in the government. The apostle Paul wrote, "Let everyone be subject to the governing authorities, for there is no authority except that which God has established. The authorities that exist have been established by God" (Romans 13:1). Any government leader who misbehaves in office must answer to the law, to the people, and ultimately to God. But you and I have a responsibility to obey the laws, pay our taxes, pray for our leaders, and treat them with respect.

The corruption we see today is nothing new. Nehemiah tells us that these same practices were common in his day in the land of Judah. But Nehemiah makes it clear that he did not participate in the greed and corruption of his predecessors. Why did he practice honest government? His motivation is clear: "But out of reverence for God I did not act like that."

Nehemiah maintained his ethical standards not merely to win favor with the people but also because he genuinely loved God. He lived out two leadership principles that Jesus gave us. One was the servanthood principle: "Whoever wants to become great among you must be your servant, and whoever wants to be first must be slave of all" (see Mark 10:43–44). The other was the gratitude principle: Jesus said, "Freely you have received; freely give" (Matthew 10:8). Gratitude to God is a powerful motivation for doing good for others. Nehemiah was grateful for all that God had done for him, and he was committed to faithfully serving God and serving the people.

Nehemiah goes on to recount:

Furthermore, a hundred and fifty Jews and officials ate at my table, as well as those who came to us from the surrounding nations. Each day one ox, six choice sheep and some poultry were prepared for me, and every ten days an abundant supply of wine of all kinds. In spite of all this, I never demanded the food allotted to the governor, because the demands were heavy on these people. (Nehemiah 5:17–18)

Here we see Nehemiah's remarkable compassion and concern for those who had less. Nehemiah was willing to provide for others at his own expense, and he permitted them to eat at his table. He was entitled by law to receive compensation—but he was constrained by his love of God to give instead. He saw that the demands were heavy on these people, so he took it upon himself to lighten their load.

Finally, he closes this account with a brief prayer: "Remember me with favor, my God, for all I have done for these people" (Nehemiah 5:19).

Prayer is characteristic of the life of Nehemiah. Some may look at this prayer and ask, "Isn't he being somewhat self-serving? Isn't he bargaining with God?" I think that's the wrong way to interpret Nehemiah's prayer. Nehemiah is recognizing God's gracious promise to care for those who walk with Him. God does not always bless us materially or financially, but He does promise to bless us when we serve Him.

This same promise is also etched into the New Testament. "God is not unjust," said the writer to the Hebrews. "He will not forget your work and the love you have shown him as you have helped his people and continue to help them" (Hebrews 6:10). We can count on this promise.

Nehemiah is not bargaining with the Lord. He is praying, in effect, "Lord, I sought to do your will. Now I pray that you will bless me according to your promise and your gracious nature." He does not bargain with God. He does not demand anything from God, nor does he ask for any specific form of blessing. He leaves that up to God. The Lord is pleased when we remember His covenant and pray according to His loving promise to bless us.

Murphy's Law was in operation long before an Air Force captain named Murphy formulated it. Murphy's Law was stirring up trouble even in Nehemiah's day. What *could* go wrong *did* go wrong during the rebuilding of the walls and gates of Jerusalem.

But God's grace and power far outweigh Murphy's Law. Whenever we face unexpected obstacles or opposition in our lives, whenever we encounter a barrier as we seek to achieve great things for God, He is present and available. His grace will always cancel out the worst that Murphy's Law can do to us.

6

††††††††††††††

DON'T VACILLATE—
PERPETUATE!

Nehemiah 6 and 7

On January 20, 1945, Franklin Delano Roosevelt was inaugurated for an unprecedented fourth term as President of the United States. His vice presidents during his first two terms had been John Nance Garner and Henry A. Wallace, but his running mate for his fourth term was a comparatively unknown senator from Missouri, Harry S. Truman. As vice president, Truman had very little contact with President Roosevelt. He was not told that Roosevelt's health was failing, nor was he allowed to take part in briefings on the progress of Allied efforts in World War II.

Just three months after the inauguration, on April 12, 1945, President Roosevelt died of a massive stroke while in Warm Springs, Georgia. Vice President Truman was as stunned as the rest of the nation when he received the news. After fewer than a hundred days as vice president, Truman found himself the chief executive of a nation at war—and he knew nothing about events on the battlefield. He was not even aware that America had a devastating secret weapon, the atomic bomb. He received a series of briefings during his first day in office, and each briefing was filled with shocking revelations of international crises and military secrets.

The day after Roosevelt's death, Truman met with reporters and said, "Boys, if you ever pray, pray for me now. I don't know if you fellas ever had a load of hay fall on you, but when they told me what happened yesterday, I felt like the moon, the stars, and all the planets had fallen on me."[1]

Our leaders need our prayers. They are dealing with issues and realities we can scarcely imagine—and the problems they face are far beyond what natural human wisdom can solve. Nothing but the supernatural wisdom of God is adequate for the job.

Many Americans assume that this nation will always be strong and will overcome any threat. But powerful empires have fallen in the past, and there are many threats to America's existence today. The national debt is a ticking time bomb that will, if not defused, blow up the world economy and devastate our society. The nations surrounding Israel continue to threaten the existence of the only democracy in the Middle East—and God's chosen people. The Soviet Union has fallen—but the Russian Empire continues to threaten world peace and stability. Terrorism is a seemingly insoluble international threat; how do you deter an enemy that would willingly kill himself in order to destroy Western civilization?

There is no guarantee that America will exist for another hundred years or even another ten years. Pray for your leaders. Pray that they would be faithful to God's Word. Pray that they would wisely seek God in all the decisions they make.

Nehemiah faced similar critical decisions as the governor of Judah and the leader of the project to rebuild the walls of Jerusalem. More than 2,500 years ago, Nehemiah faced crises and problems that threatened the existence of the Jewish state—problems that still confront the Jewish state today. By examining his story, by studying his approaches to problem-solving, we will learn how to rebuild our own lives and repair the weak areas where we are vulnerable to attack.

One of the crucial lessons of the book of Nehemiah is that life is a battle from beginning to end. From the moment he set his heart to obey God's command and rebuild the city defenses, Nehemiah found himself exposed to attack. Nehemiah's opponents began plotting against him even before he reached Jerusalem. And once he arrived, his enemies arose in force.

Know Your Enemy

You may not have experienced opposition for doing God's will—but if you live obediently for God, you can count on it, opposition will come. And the ultimate source of that opposition is not mere human anger or hate. As Paul told the Christians in Ephesus, "For our struggle is not against flesh and blood, but against the rulers, against the authorities, against the powers of this dark world and against the spiritual forces of evil in the heavenly realms" (Ephesians 6:12).

People are not the problem. When people attack us, we easily assume they are the enemy. But our real enemy is invisible. Our enemy strikes us from the spiritual realm—and he uses people as his weapons against us. The rulers and authorities and powers of this dark world are active today, just as they fiercely opposed Nehemiah in his day. Our enemy loves to lie and kill and demoralize us whenever we set out to do God's work. That is the battle we face. And that battle will continue throughout our lives.

Throughout Scripture, and especially here in Nehemiah, we see that the devil has two primary forms of attack. We need to keep these satanic strategies in mind, because we will encounter them again and again throughout our lives. We need to know who and what we are fighting, and how our enemy operates.

First, Satan comes at us with the ferocity of a ravenous beast. The apostle Peter wrote, "Be alert and of sober mind. Your enemy the devil prowls around like a roaring lion looking for someone to devour" (1 Peter 5:8). A lion is an incredibly powerful and dangerous animal. His jaws are so strong that he can crush the thickest bone in the human body, the thighbone. One blow from a lion's paw can smash a human skull like an eggshell. Peter wants us to know that Satan seeks to attack us with calamity and disaster. He seeks to destroy us physically, emotionally, relationally, and spiritually.

Second, Satan also approaches us in disguise—in a form the apostle Paul calls "an angel of light" (see 2 Corinthians 11:14). He comes to us with the appearance of wisdom, gentleness, compassion, charm, and attractiveness—and he offers enticing promises and flattering words. Satan assures us that the things he tempts us with will grant us everything and cost us nothing.

Down through history, false prophets have led millions astray. False political leaders have plunged the world into war and chaos. False teachers have peddled their false gospels to the gullible through TV shows and best-selling books. At first, they all look like angels of light. They are attractive and charming. Their words are soothing and persuasive. And like the Pied Piper of the ancient tale, they lead their followers to destruction.

How do we avoid being taken in by Satan, the false "angel of light," and his human agents of deception? Paul says we should live godly lives "in order that Satan might not outwit us. For we are not unaware of his schemes" (2 Corinthians 2:11). And here in

Nehemiah 6, we learn from Nehemiah himself how to be on guard against the devil and his schemes.

In the first five chapters of Nehemiah, we have seen Nehemiah's enemies using the first form of satanic attack—a frontal assault, the devouring beast approach. But in Nehemiah 6, his enemies switch to the second form of satanic attack—they employ charm and persuasion against Nehemiah. They present themselves as agents of the "angel of light."

In chapter 6, following a series of attacks and threats against Nehemiah in an effort to intimidate him, Nehemiah's enemies abruptly change their tactics. They resort to friendliness and persuasion.

> When word came to Sanballat, Tobiah, Geshem the Arab and the rest of our enemies that I had rebuilt the wall and not a gap was left in it—though up to that time I had not set the doors in the gates—Sanballat and Geshem sent me this message: "Come, let us meet together in one of the villages on the plain of Ono."
>
> But they were scheming to harm me; so I sent messengers to them with this reply: "I am carrying on a great project and cannot go down. Why should the work stop while I leave it and go down to you?" Four times they sent me the same message, and each time I gave them the same answer. (vv. 1–4)

God's enemies could not halt the reconstruction project by threat and attack, so they switched tactics. You will often find, when you seek to do God's will, that sometimes your enemy will try to defeat you and destroy you—and sometimes your enemy will try to charm you and win you over. Some of the most winsome and friendly people in your life might well be your most bitter enemies—if you could only see inside their hearts. They may even think they are doing you a favor by persuading you to try this kind of behavior or that kind of belief system. Their words sound like good advice, and it seems to make sense while they are talking to you—but if you check everything they say against the wisdom of Scripture, you may find that it doesn't add up.

Nehemiah's enemies did a turnabout and presented themselves as friends. They invited Nehemiah to a conference on the Plain of Ono. (The Plain of Ono is where the Ben Gurion Airport is today, near Tel Aviv.) In fact, they asked him to meet with them not once, but four times.

Nehemiah knew that his enemies were scheming to cause him harm, so he refused to attend the meeting on the plain. What was the nature of their scheme? We don't know. Some Bible commentators suggest that this was a ploy to lure Nehemiah out of the city, where he had plenty of bodyguards, and out onto the plain where he would be exposed to an ambush. Nehemiah flatly refused to go.

It's important to note the reasons Nehemiah gave for not going. At first, this seems like a surly and ill-tempered response to their invitation: "I am carrying on a great project and cannot go down. Why should the work stop while I leave it and go down to you?" But Nehemiah is not merely being rude. He is stating the essential reason for his refusal: he was doing a great work in which he was pursuing a great calling from God himself, so he refused to be distracted from his goal.

Many of us have a hard time saying no to people who intrude on our time. We feel obligated to attend this function or that meeting, even though it is going to take us away from the important work God has given us to do. We need to keep our priorities straight. Keep your focus on what is truly important in life. Stand steady and firm under pressure, even if people repeatedly try to pull you away from God's work.

At the same time, we need to be sensitive to "the ministry of interruptions." Jesus often allowed himself to be interrupted by an urgent human need—someone who needed to be healed, some-one who needed the gospel. But Jesus refused to be diverted and distracted by the opposition of the Pharisees and other pointless demands on His time. He stayed focused on His goals, including the goal of ministering to people in need.

I once read of a young missionary in China prior to World War II. He was a recent university graduate just twenty-eight years old, fluent in Mandarin Chinese and a proven leader. An American oil company wanted to open a new operation in China, and it planned to open its main office in the city where this young man lived. When company officials became aware of this young mis-sionary, they offered him a position with their company at ten times the amount of money he was allowed as a missionary. The oil company executives were shocked when he turned down their generous offer.

So the officials came back with a much larger offer. He turned that offer down as well. So they came back a third time with an even bigger salary offer. Again, he declined. Finally the executives asked him, "What will you take?"

"You don't understand," the missionary said. "It's not that the salary is too little. It's that the job is too small."

We are easily lured away from God's will by the offer of money or some other worldly inducement. We rationalize and tell ourselves, "My motives are godly. There is so much good I can do if I only had more money, more this or more that." So instead of taking on the big job God wants us to do, we accept the much smaller job that pays bigger money or that offers bigger worldly inducements.

No matter what self-deceptive rationalizations we use, God isn't deceived. He knows that our true motives are self-serving, not God-serving. And He won't bless the work we do that is outside of His will. That's why Nehemiah tells his foes that he is engaged in a great work, fulfilling a calling that God himself has given to him. He will not forsake that work for anything less.

Years ago, Bible teacher F. B. Meyer wrote a commentary on Nehemiah's reply in Nehemiah 6:3:

> It was a sublime answer. Below was the Plain of Ono, where Nehemiah's foes awaited him. Let him once descend into it and he would become their easy prey; but he withstood their four-fold solicitation by considering the greatness of the work he was doing and the responsible position he was called to fill. Other-worldliness is the best cure for worldliness. . . .
>
> Oh, children of the Great King, let us pray that we may know the grandeur of our position before Him; the high calling with which we have been called; the vast responsibilities with which we are entrusted; the great work of co-operating with God in erecting the city of God. Heirs of God and joint-heirs with Christ! Called to sit with Christ in the Heavenlies! Risen, ascended, crowned in Him! Sitting with Christ, far above all principality and power! How can we go down—down to the world that rejected Him; down to the level of the first Adam, from which, at so great cost, we have been raised . . . !
>
> As we make our choice, let us look to the living and ascended Christ to make it good. Put your will on his side, and expect that the energy of the power that raised Him from the dead will raise and maintain you in union with Him.[2]

Nehemiah was confronted with an offer that seemed to promise peace and support—yet that offer was as deceptive as the "gift" of a wooden horse the Greeks presented to Troy after a failed military siege. The Trojans pulled the horse into their city as a trophy of victory—and in the middle of the night, Greek soldiers emerged from the horse, opened the city gates, and allowed the Greek army to enter and defeat the Trojans.[3]

Nehemiah's enemies attempted to deceive Nehemiah with a "Trojan horse" offer of their own. But Nehemiah refused the "gift horse" that was offered to him. He had more important work to do.

The Attacks Continue

When the enemy cannot accomplish his purpose by direct assault, he will often try to win through deception by offering peace and friendship. And if the false offer of peace fails, the enemy will often return to his original strategy of direct attack. Nehemiah 6 records:

Then, the fifth time, Sanballat sent his aide to me with the same message, and in his hand was an unsealed letter in which was written:

"It is reported among the nations—and Geshem says it is true—that you and the Jews are plotting to revolt, and therefore you are building the wall. Moreover, according to these reports you are about to become their king and have even appointed prophets to make this proclamation about you in Jerusalem: 'There is a king in Judah!' Now this report will get back to the king; so come, let us meet together."

I sent him this reply: "Nothing like what you are saying is happening; you are just making it up out of your head." (vv. 5–8)

This arm-twisting tactic was designed to put pressure on Nehemiah. If they could maneuver Nehemiah into their trap, they would be able to destroy him. But Nehemiah saw this ploy for what it was: an enticement based on lies and motivated by hate. He responded with a simple refusal.

I'm reminded of the anonymous complaint letters that pastors inevitably receive. My practice was always to toss such letters in the wastebasket. I saw no reason to consider the complaints of those who lack the courage to sign their letters. After all, what sort of retaliation were they expecting from their pastor that they would be afraid to sign their own name? If anyone wanted to discuss one of my sermons or one of my decisions as pastor, I would have gladly and cordially done so, and even if we disagreed, we would have still been friends.

I once heard about a man who was speaking before an audience, and someone in the audience passed a note up to the platform. The speaker stopped his speech, unfolded the note, and saw that it only had one word written on it—"Fool." The speaker turned to the audience and said, "I have received many unsigned messages before, but this is the first time I ever received a note from someone who signed his name but forgot to write a message."

Nehemiah makes a point of the fact that the letter he received was unsealed. A sealed letter would be addressed to Nehemiah alone. An unsealed letter was an open letter designed by the sender to be read by everyone involved in its delivery. In other words, the sender, Sanballat, intended that the contents of the letter be spread as far and wide as possible. He was deliberately spreading the lie that Nehemiah was a rebel who was trying to make himself king.

Notice Nehemiah's response: simple denial. Nehemiah does not attempt to disprove the accusation and prove his own innocence. He simply calls the accusation a lie, unworthy of a detailed rebuttal. Then Nehemiah takes the matter to God in prayer: "They were all trying to frighten us, thinking, 'Their hands will get too weak for the work, and it will not be completed.'

"But I prayed, 'Now strengthen my hands'" (v. 9).

Nehemiah's enemies wanted to plant the suspicion in the minds of the people that Nehemiah was seeking his own glory by rebuilding the wall. Sanballat, Geshem, and the other opponents of this effort hoped to demoralize the workers so they would quit. So Nehemiah prayed, in effect, "Lord, do not let that happen. Strengthen me to work all the harder."

Whenever we are attacked with lies and attempts to undermine our morale, our first response must be to drop to our knees and lay the matter before the Lord in prayer. That's the example Nehemiah leaves as his legacy, both as a leader and a servant of God.

Having failed yet again to trap or trick Nehemiah, his enemies switch to yet another form of subterfuge:

> One day I went to the house of Shemaiah son of Delaiah, the son of Mehetabel, who was shut in at his home. He said, "Let us meet in the house of God, inside the temple, and let us close the temple doors, because men are coming to kill you—by night they are coming to kill you." (v. 10)

This word comes in the form of a prophecy—but this man Shemaiah is a *false* prophet. He claims to have hidden knowledge, perhaps occult knowledge, suggested by the fact that he "was shut in at his home." This does not mean he was sick or infirm. In the original language, this suggests that, for some religious reason, he kept himself in seclusion. This is frequently the case with those who claim to be in touch with the "spirit world." Their seclusion behind curtains and clouds of incense helps to maintain an air of mystery.

What Shemaiah says sounds logical. He said, in effect, "Some men are coming to kill you—let me protect you. We will go into the temple, shut the doors, and no one will dare to attack you there." Nehemiah instantly senses a trap. Only priests are permitted to enter the temple—and Nehemiah was not a priest. He was not going to violate God's ordinances to save his life. He refused Shemaiah's offer: "But I said, 'Should a man like me run away? Or should someone like me go into the temple to save his life? I will not go!'" (v. 11).

Nehemiah knew that a prophet who is truly from the Lord would not say anything that violates the ordinances of God. There was an altar of asylum in the temple courtyard, and people were permitted to flee to the courtyard and be safe—but that's not what Shemaiah proposed. He urged Nehemiah to go into the temple building itself and shut the doors.

Clearly, Shemaiah was trying at the very least to discredit Nehemiah by enticing him into violating God's commandments. In fact, Shemaiah might have been trying to lure him into an ambush as well. Nehemiah's enemies could say, "Well, Nehemiah was ambushed and murdered—but he was violating God's laws, so he got what he deserved." I don't know whether Nehemiah simply knew better than to walk into their trap or he was warned by the Spirit of God. In any case, he avoided Shemaiah's trap:

> I realized that God had not sent him, but that he had prophesied against me because Tobiah and Sanballat had hired him. He had been hired to intimidate me so that I would commit a sin by doing this, and then they would give me a bad name to discredit me. (vv. 12–13)

Nehemiah demonstrated the wisdom of a godly leader by not falling for the tricks and enticements of his enemies. These godless men, motivated by jealousy and ambition, did everything they could think of to destroy Nehemiah. They tried to physically take his life. They tried to destroy his reputation. They tried to destroy the trust his people had in him. They tried to undermine his efforts by demoralizing the people. Nothing worked, because Nehemiah relied on God to elude their attacks.

Nehemiah's real enemy, of course, was Satan—the same enemy you and I confront in our lives today. Whenever we are attacked by godless people, we must remember that our real enemy is not flesh and blood. Our mortal enemy is a spiritual foe.

Remember too that Satan will sometimes attack us through people we think are our friends. They may give us advice that violates the

Word of God. They may be well-intentioned or ill-intentioned. People who do Satan's bidding often don't realize they are doing so. Many people give ungodly advice with the best of intentions but with the worst discernment and a lack of biblical wisdom.

Don't be fooled by someone's supposed "good intentions." Test the advice people give you against God's infallible Word. That is what Nehemiah does here. He replies, "Should a man like me run away? Or should someone like me go into the temple to save his life? I will not go!" (v. 11).

Nehemiah knows who he is. He is a servant of the living God, and a servant always obeys his Master. And since God has decreed that only priests may enter the temple building, Nehemiah refuses to disobey his Master and resort to ungodly means to save his life.

The New Testament calls us to the same way of life that Nehemiah exemplifies. The apostle Paul tells us that amid all the problems and pressures of life we must live as servants of the living God—obedient to our Master. Paul urges us "to live lives worthy of God, who calls you into his kingdom and glory" (1 Thessalonians 2:12).

We are God's children and we are God's servants, and we belong to Him. Therefore, we must live on a different moral and ethical plane than the people around us. We cannot use ungodly methods, even to do what seems good and expedient. We cannot resort to worldly practices even to save our lives. We cannot give in to the peer pressure and enticements of this world in order to "fit in." God never calls us to "fit in" with this ungodly world; He calls us to stand out, to be distinct, to not be conformed to the pattern of this dying world.

In *Walden*, Henry David Thoreau wrote, "If a man does not keep pace with his companions, perhaps it is because he hears a different drummer. Let him step to the music which he hears, however measured or far away."[4] Christians should not keep pace with the world. We should always keep our ears tuned to the beat of a different

Drummer. We should always keep in step with His music, not the music of the world.

Nothing will free us more from the subtle pressures and temptations of today than to remember who we are. We are in this world, not of it. This world has been enslaved by Satan, the god of this world—but we Christians are servants of a different Master. If you know who you are as a child of the King, you will not be deceived by Satan.

Nehemiah knew who he was, and he knew God's purpose for his life—and in this way he avoided the traps of his enemies. Nehemiah also prayed that God would intervene in his circumstances and deal with these enemies who tried to trap him: "Remember Tobiah and Sanballat, my God, because of what they have done; remember also the prophet Noadiah and how she and the rest of the prophets have been trying to intimidate me" (Nehemiah 6:14).

Here, Nehemiah refers to a woman named Noadiah, a false prophet who has been a ringleader of a group of prophets who attempted to demoralize and intimidate Nehemiah. He asks God to be his vindicator against those who have opposed his work. Nehemiah relies on the righteous judgment and invisible hand of God.

We too need to rely on God as our defender and vindicator. When we face opposition and hostility from the enemies of God, we need to remember that the Word of God and the Spirit of God were given to guide us and comfort us through our trials—and to show us how to respond under pressure. The same resources Nehemiah relied on are available to us today.

The Unending Struggle

This brings us to the end of this first phase of Nehemiah's work.

So the wall was completed on the twenty-fifth of Elul, in fifty-two days. When all our enemies heard about this, all the surrounding nations were afraid and lost their self-confidence, because they realized that this work had been done with the help of our God. (Nehemiah 6:15–16)

Even the enemies of Israel, the enemies of God, had to admit that God was at work in the lives of His people. The people of Jerusalem achieved amazing success, completing the entire project in a mere fifty-two days. Rebuilding the walls and gates of Jerusalem in less than two months was an amazing accomplishment—a feat that could have only been achieved by *supernatural* power.

Nehemiah had left Persia in April, and it took him several months to journey to Jerusalem. By October 2 in 445 BC the wall was completed. The people finished the work in fifty-two days because they put their minds and their shoulders to the task, and they looked to God for the wisdom and power to achieve it.

The result? Nehemiah's enemies heard of the achievement—and they lost all their swagger and arrogance. They realized they had been battling God himself. Who can hope to overcome the power of the One who created the universe?

This is a beautiful picture of the power of Christian witness in a community of faith. When God's enemies—the secularists, the atheists, the cultists, the false religionists—see the power of God at work in our midst, they must confess that our God is at work among us.

This doesn't mean that all of God's opponents will come to their senses and come to faith in Him. Some may, but most will still oppose God and hate His people. In fact, they will become angrier and more hostile in defeat. They will continue their tactics of opposition—but at least for the moment, they'll be forced to acknowledge that the power of Almighty God has dealt them a setback.

In the closing verses of Nehemiah 6, we see how God's defeated enemies refuse to give up but continue their tactics of opposition:

Also, in those days the nobles of Judah were sending many letters to Tobiah, and replies from Tobiah kept coming to them. For many in Judah were under oath to him, since he was son-in-law to Shekaniah son of Arah, and his son Jehohanan had married the daughter of Meshullam son of Berekiah. Moreover, they kept reporting to me his good deeds and then telling him what I said. And Tobiah sent letters to intimidate me. (vv. 17–19)

Tobiah and his son Jehohanan had intermarried with the Israelites. Taking advantage of that relationship, Tobiah tried to undermine Nehemiah's influence and destroy his reputation with gossip. Here's an important lesson for our lives today: Satan never quits. As long as we live and serve God, he is never going to give up. He will continue to wage war until he is finally vanquished and consigned to the lake of fire.

The battle against Satan has been as intense in the later years of my life as it was in the early years. I do not expect Satan to relent in his fight against me until the Lord calls me to glory. That is the nature of the Christian life. It is, as Paul has said, a good fight. But it is a fight.

You can retire from a job or career, but you can never retire from the spiritual battlefield. God has many wonderful blessings and joys for us along the way, but as long as we have breath, we must never cease to fight this good battle against the world, the flesh, and the devil. That is the lesson of Nehemiah 6.

Perpetuating the Legacy

Nehemiah 7 is the longest chapter in the book. It is largely a list of the families who had been exiled in Babylon and were now permitted to return to their homeland. I will not include the full text of Nehemiah 7 in these pages. The theme of this chapter could be summarized as: "Nehemiah leaves a legacy."

As a leader, he has organized and motivated the people to achieve a great victory—the reconstruction of the city walls and gates in the face of enormous opposition. Now he seeks to perpetuate that victory and leave a legacy by appointing wise successors and establishing enduring policies. He writes:

> After the wall had been rebuilt and I had set the doors in place, the gatekeepers, the musicians and the Levites were appointed. I put in charge of Jerusalem my brother Hanani, along with Hananiah the commander of the citadel, because he was a man of integrity and feared God more than most people do. I said to them, "The gates of Jerusalem are not to be opened until the sun is hot. While the gatekeepers are still on duty, have them shut the doors and bar them. Also appoint residents of Jerusalem as guards, some at their posts and some near their own houses." (vv. 1–3)

The wall was complete—but the battle was not over. Nehemiah continued to take precautions against further attack. He knew that his enemies had not given up their quest to render Jerusalem helpless once more. In those days, walled cities would open their gates at dawn so merchants and traders could come and go. But Nehemiah ordered that Jerusalem keep its gates shut until the heat of the day, when the sun beat down upon the land. This would preclude any possibility of a surprise attack while the people were still sleeping. He also appointed citizens of Jerusalem as guards who were posted at strategic points along the city wall.

Now, all of these are practical considerations for a city ringed by enemies. Yet these precautions also have symbolic value for our lives today. They teach us that we must never let our guard down. Many Christian leaders have fallen into disgrace during their later years because they let their guard down and failed to do battle with the enemy of their soul.

The rest of Nehemiah 7 is concerned with preserving the purity of the doctrine God had entrusted to the people of Israel. It was necessary to ensure that only true Israelites lived within the walls of Jerusalem. Nehemiah writes:

> Now the city was large and spacious, but there were few people in it, and the houses had not yet been rebuilt. So my God put it into my heart to assemble the nobles, the officials and the common people for registration by families. I found the genealogical record of those who had been the first to return. This is what I found written there. (vv. 4–5)

After this comes a list of the names of all the families who returned to Jerusalem from Persian-controlled Babylon under the leadership of Ezra. That return took place some thirty years before the time of Nehemiah. The people on this list are the ones, of course, who helped Nehemiah rebuild the wall. Here, Nehemiah not only gives credit to them but also recognizes that they will be responsible for carrying on the work he has begun. So, having appointed leaders who would succeed him—people of integrity, courage, and faithfulness—Nehemiah sees to it that those who come after them are true Israelites.

The list of families who are able to prove their ancestry is found in Nehemiah 7:6–60. Is there a spiritual application of this long list of names we can make to our lives today? Yes, and the application is this: We need to know that we truly belong to God. We can never be successful servants of Christ until we are assured that we know Him and belong to Him. In order to be effective for God, we must know our spiritual pedigree.

In Nehemiah 7:61–62, Nehemiah lists a number of people who came from towns in the surrounding region and were not able to show that their families were truly descended from Israel. Because of their uncertain ancestry, they were not permitted to live within the city of Jerusalem.

Next, in Nehemiah 7:63–65, Nehemiah purified the rolls of the priesthood, removing any priests who could not prove their lineage. These were not allowed to eat of the sacred temple food "until there should be a priest ministering with the Urim and Thummim" (v. 65). There is a lesson in these verses for us today. Many people in the church presume to minister in God's name when they themselves do not have a real relationship with Jesus Christ. They are not true Christians, and they are not authentic ministers of the gospel. They often wreak havoc in the church.

Nehemiah's reference to the Urim and Thummim is interesting. These are the names of two precious stones worn by the high priest on his priestly garments. The name Urim means "Lights." The name Thummim means "Perfections." The high priest was able to use these stones to determine the will of God. No one knows how the stones were used. The Scriptures do not tell us how the stones revealed God's will. Nehemiah says that the priests who could not prove their lineage were disqualified. They were not allowed to minister until a high priest arrived who had the Urim and Thummim.

I have a theory—and it's only a theory. I can't prove it. But I think that reference to the high priest who possesses the Urim and Thummim is a prophetic reference to our Lord Jesus. In the book of Hebrews, Jesus is said to be "high priest in the order of Melchizedek" (Hebrews 5:10). In other words, Jesus is a priest who lives forever and who fully knows the mind of God. He can restore a disqualified priest to a place of ministry and give him back his priestly office.

How do we apply this principle to our lives today? What is today's equivalent of a disqualified priest, a priest of uncertain lineage? Who is the disqualified priest who Jesus can restore to a priestly ministry? I believe that you and I are the disqualified priests. All

Christians are disqualified priests who have been restored to our priestly office by Jesus Christ.

One of the fundamental truths of our faith is that every believer is a priest. The apostle Peter tells us that we are a royal priesthood in a priestly kingdom (see 1 Peter 2:9). The Scriptures also tell us that through His blood the Lord Jesus Christ has made us priests and kings (see Revelation 5:10). Jesus is our High Priest, and He knows the mind of God. It is He who has restored us to our priestly office when we had lost the right to serve as priests.

The closing verses of Nehemiah 7 tell us of a number of people who returned to Jerusalem and of a great offering that was taken for the rebuilding of the walls. It also tells us how the suburbs of the city were settled.

Nehemiah 6 opened with an account of all the pressures and temptations Nehemiah faced as his enemies tried to prevent him from completing his task. Nehemiah 7 closes this section of the account by listing the results of his success. He stood firm against the pressures and temptations of his day—and we need to stand firm against the pressures and temptations that come our way. The same satanic will that opposed Nehemiah still opposes us today. And we can overcome Satan's schemes the same way Nehemiah overcame his enemies.

First, Nehemiah understood the magnitude and importance of the task God had given him—and he refused to let threats and opposition pull him off course. He stayed focused on his God-given priorities, and he completed his mission.

Second, Nehemiah never forgot his identity. He knew who he was—a servant of the Lord God. He knew he belonged to God and that God had called him to lead His people in rebuilding the city.

Third, Nehemiah was immune to the pressure and temptation of his enemies. He was even immune to the enticements of so-called "friends" who actually wanted to defeat and destroy him. He refused to accept the counsel of those who had worldly motives and who lacked the wisdom of God. He never vacillated—he persevered and perpetuated the work he had begun.

Fourth, Nehemiah was a practical man who is not only deeply spiritual but he also possessed practical common sense. He investigated and assessed the situation, organized the people, set up guards, assigned responsibilities, and shared the labor. He was not merely a great spiritual leader—though he was every bit of that. He was also a great motivator, organizer, analyzer, and construction boss.

Fifth, Nehemiah was a man of prayer. He subjected everything to the wisdom of God. I probably should have listed the prayerfulness of Nehemiah first, because he always began with prayer. But the prayerfulness of Nehemiah is so important that I wanted to leave it with you as the concluding thought of this chapter.

Begin and end every project, every leadership challenge, every mission for God with prayer. Don't attempt anything until you have sought the mind of God. Don't merely ask God to bless what you have already decided to do—seek His will, first and foremost.

The story of Nehemiah is a practical illustration of one of the great truths of Scripture—a passage I memorized early in my life, one I have relied on countless times in countless situations: "Trust in the LORD with all thine heart; and lean not unto thine own understanding. In all thy ways acknowledge him, and he shall direct thy paths" (Proverbs 3:5–6 KJV).

If you want God to crown your life with success, if you want to accomplish great things for Him, then begin every day and every task with prayer. Trust in Him, and He will direct and guide you throughout your life.

7

†††††††††††††††

REDISCOVERING GOD'S HIDDEN RICHES

Nehemiah 8

A number of years ago, in the days before email, a Christian father was preparing his son to embark on his freshman year at Duke University. "Son," he said, "I want you to have this Bible. In it you'll find all the riches of God's wisdom for every situation you face."

The young man took the Bible and placed it in his suitcase. He said goodbye to his parents, got in his car, and took off for college. Weeks passed, and the young man finally wrote to his parents, telling them he needed money and to please send a check.

The father wrote back, "Son, I'm not enclosing a check. Instead, I encourage you to read your Bible." And he suggested the specific Scripture passage to read.

The young man wrote again, saying, "Dad, I am reading my Bible—but I really need that money. Please send!"

Well, this father and his son exchanged several letters, and the father steadfastly refused to send a check, and the son's pleas for money grew more and more urgent and insistent. The son said he was reading his Bible, but his needs were financial, not spiritual.

Finally, the young man came home for a semester break, and he was upset with his father for not sending a check. The father said, "Son, you never needed any money. All the money you needed, you already had—you just didn't know it. You kept telling me you were reading your Bible—but I knew you weren't. If you had opened your Bible to the Scripture verses I sent you, then you would have found the cash I had tucked into the pages at those verses."

God's Word is a rich and rewarding source of wisdom for our lives—and God has tucked His riches into its pages for our use. But we can't take advantage of those riches if we never open those pages. That's the lesson of Nehemiah 8.

Nehemiah accomplished an amazing task in leading the rebuilding of the walls and gates of Jerusalem. Here, in Nehemiah 8, we see that after the reconstruction we need reinstruction. We need to change the way we think about ourselves and about all of life.

Few of us realize how much we have been affected and infected by the deceptive philosophies of this world. We have picked up attitudes, ideas, and assumptions that we don't even realize are wrong and unchristian. So we need to be reinstructed in God's view of life. As we approach the eighth chapter of Nehemiah, I'm reminded of the words of the apostle Peter:

> For this very reason, make every effort to add to your faith goodness; and to goodness, knowledge; and to knowledge, self-control; and to self-control, perseverance; and to perseverance, godliness;

and to godliness, mutual affection; and to mutual affection, love. (2 Peter 1:5–7)

We all need to be reinstructed in the qualities that lead to lasting wholeness. Brokenness results from forgetting God's Word and living like the rest of the world. Wholeness comes from rediscovering God's Word and becoming distinct and separate from the world. As the apostle Paul wrote: "Do not conform to the pattern of this world, but be transformed by the renewing of your mind. Then you will be able to test and approve what God's will is—his good, pleasing and perfect will" (Romans 12:2).

The only way to renew our minds is by immersing ourselves in the Word of God. If you need to change things in your life (or you are praying for someone else who does), then change must come through the knowledge of the Word of God, through an understanding of God's truth. That is why this key chapter, Nehemiah 8, opens with a manifestation of a great hunger for the Word of God among the people of Jerusalem.

A Hunger for the Word of God

The last part of the last verse of Nehemiah 7 actually belongs with Nehemiah 8. Although the Word of God is divinely inspired, the chapter and verse divisions are not. So we will begin our journey through Nehemiah 8 with the closing words of Nehemiah 7:

When the seventh month came and the Israelites had settled in their towns, all the people came together as one in the square before the Water Gate. They told Ezra the teacher of the Law to bring out the Book of the Law of Moses, which the LORD had commanded for Israel.

So on the first day of the seventh month Ezra the priest brought the Law before the assembly, which was made up of men and women and all who were able to understand. He read it aloud from day-break till noon as he faced the square before the Water Gate in the presence of the men, women and others who could understand. And all the people listened attentively to the Book of the Law. (Nehemiah 7:73–8:3)

This seems to be a spontaneous gathering. Nehemiah tells us that "all the people came together as one." No invitations were sent out. No public notice was given. People came together because they were hungry for answers to their problems, for guidelines from the Word of God. So they all gathered in the great square before the Water Gate.

The people asked Ezra the priest to bring the Law of God and read it to them. This would undoubtedly be the entire Pentateuch—the first five books of the Bible: Genesis, Exodus, Leviticus, Numbers, and Deuteronomy. This indicates the tremendous desire of these people for truth. They listened, while standing, from daybreak until noon. Why were they able to maintain such a long attention span? Undoubtedly, this indicates that the people were deeply and pain-fully conscious of their ignorance about God's will for their lives and for their nation. They were crying out for the Word.

Notice that the date of this great assembly was "the first day of the seventh month" (8:2) on the Hebrew calendar, which would be October 8, 445 BC. Notice also that Ezra the priest, the author of the book of Ezra, appears here for the first time in the book of Nehemiah. Thirteen years earlier he had led a return from Persia to rebuild the temple and teach the Law of God. He was probably occupied in that task throughout the time of the rebuilding of the wall. Now that the work is finished, the people were desperate to hear from God's Word. So they sent for Ezra to read to them from the Scriptures.

Notice, also, that the people gathered before the Water Gate. As we have already seen when we looked at Nehemiah 3, this gate symbolizes the Word of God—the water of the Word. There could be no more appropriate place for the people to assemble. The congregation included men, women, and children who were of an age to understand. All were hungry for God's Word.

Today, it seems that there is very little hunger for God's Word. Yet the prophet Amos predicted that there would come a time of famine in the world—not a famine for food, but a famine for the Word of God. It would be a time when people would be starving for answers to the problems of life. Such days, I believe, are still ahead of us. When people are well fed, well clothed, when the economy is doing fine and the world is comparatively peaceful, people feel little need of God and His Word.

But when wars, terror attacks, financial upheaval, plagues, and racial violence strike fear into the hearts of people, they sometimes turn for answers to the Word of God. Even now, whenever the Bible is proclaimed without compromise, but with clarity and understanding, people are drawn to it. God's Word throws open the gates of the human heart so the Holy Spirit can come in—bringing conviction and cleansing.

Some years ago, I was invited to speak to a group of Chinese professionals in Singapore. About four dozen doctors, lawyers, educators, and engineers met on an upper level of a high-rise apartment building in the city. As I opened the Bible and began to speak, I discovered that these people, most of them nonbelievers, were fascinated by God's Word. Their faces shone with curiosity and enthusiasm, and they asked question after question.

When it was time for me to leave for another appointment, many of them crowded into the elevator with me, and others took other elevators to meet me in the lobby. They asked questions all the way out onto the street. Even as I got into the car and pulled away from the curb, they were still shouting questions to me.

I have never forgotten that amazing display of hunger for God's Word among people who had never been taught the Scriptures before. When the Word is opened and expounded to people, it provokes a hunger. That is the power of Scripture.

One of the great tragedies of our time is how few churches and individual Christians seem to appreciate the power of the Word of God. Across this country and around the world, there are thousands of churches that show few signs of life. Their worship services are dull and dreary because the Word of God is not central to the life of those churches. We who believe in the power of God's Word need to pray for a renewed hunger for God's truth in our society—and in our churches.

Small Group Bible Studies

The Word of God is the sole attraction at this gathering. Ezra does not need to hire a rock band or cater a barbecue to attract a crowd and hold their attention. The Word of God alone compels the people to stand and listen:

> Ezra the teacher of the Law stood on a high wooden platform built for the occasion. Beside him on his right stood Mattithiah, Shema, Anaiah, Uriah, Hilkiah and Maaseiah; and on his left were Pedaiah, Mishael, Malkijah, Hashum, Hashbaddanah, Zechariah and Meshullam.
>
> Ezra opened the book. All the people could see him because he was standing above them; and as he opened it, the people all stood up. Ezra praised the LORD, the great God; and all the people lifted their hands and responded, "Amen! Amen!" Then they bowed down and worshiped the LORD with their faces to the ground. (Nehemiah 8:4–6)

Nehemiah gives us an eyewitness account of this amazing assembly. His account reminds me of some churches I have visited in Scotland. Scottish churches have high pulpits, like the pulpit from which Ezra read the Word of God. To step into the pulpit of those churches, you often have to ascend twenty or thirty steps. It is a remarkable experience to look out across a congregation that is far below you, looking up at you.

Scottish churches have a unique worship ceremony. An officer of the Church of Scotland, called the Beadle, comes down the aisle with an open Bible in his hand and the congregation stands. The Beadle places the Bible on the pulpit, and the people say, "Amen! Amen!" I believe this Scottish worship tradition is derived from this account in Nehemiah.

Next, we learn how careful the people were to make sure they understood the true meaning of the Scripture text that was read to them:

> The Levites—Jeshua, Bani, Sherebiah, Jamin, Akkub, Shabbethai, Hodiah, Maaseiah, Kelita, Azariah, Jozabad, Hanan and Pelaiah— instructed the people in the Law while the people were standing there. They read from the Book of the Law of God, making it clear and giving the meaning so that the people understood what was being read. (vv. 7–8)

This is an abundantly clear statement on how a church service ought to be conducted. The primary business of Christians is to understand the Word of God, so they will be able to think God's thoughts after Him. In other words, our goal should be to *learn to think like God.*

What does Nehemiah mean when he says that the Levites were instructing the people in the Law, reading from the Book of the Law, and making the meaning clear to the people? Some Bible scholars have suggested that the Levites were translating the Scriptures from the Hebrew language to Aramaic. I doubt that this is the case.

Hebrew and Aramaic were very similar languages, and it's unlikely that the people would need a translation.

Instead, I believe (and some Bible scholars agree) that these Levites were among the people, breaking the crowd down into smaller groups where people could ask questions and their questions could be answered. They would listen to Ezra read from the high pulpit, and then they would discuss God's Word in small groups. The Levites would pass among these groups, offering commentary and answering questions. In fact, these might well have been the first small group Bible studies in history.

To this day, this remains one of the most effective models for encouraging biblical understanding and spiritual maturity in the church: small groups of believers, studying God's Word together, applying the Scriptures to their everyday lives, and praying for one another on a regular basis.

The Joy of the Lord Is Your Strength

Next, we see Nehemiah, Ezra, and the Levites dealing with the emotional impact of God's Word on the people:

> Then Nehemiah the governor, Ezra the priest and teacher of the Law, and the Levites who were instructing the people said to them all, "This day is holy to the LORD your God. Do not mourn or weep." For all the people had been weeping as they listened to the words of the Law. (v. 9)

Why did the people weep? They wept because the Word of God had a profound impact on their souls, their spirit, and their emotions. Until they heard God's Word read to them, they didn't realize how far they had strayed from God's standard for their lives. As they listened, they realized what had caused the ruin and destruction in their lives. They realized that the city had been destroyed and the nation laid waste because of the sin of the people.

Through the reading of the Law, they finally saw the beauty of God contrasted with the ugliness of humanity and human sin. They were stricken in their own hearts—their own consciences—and they realized the suffering they had inflicted on themselves and their children through their sin and rebellion. That is always the ministry of Scripture to the human heart.

God always lays the weakness and folly of the world at the door of believers, for it is we who should be instructing the people of this fallen world. When the church does not understand its own sin and folly, it cannot challenge the sin and folly of the world. The Lord Jesus put it this way: "What comes out of a person is what defiles them. For it is from within, out of a person's heart, that evil thoughts come—sexual immorality, theft, murder, adultery, greed, malice, deceit, lewdness, envy, slander, arrogance and folly" (Mark 7:20–22).

All of these sins come from within. The hearing of the Word of God forces us to recognize the sin and corruption that defiles us from within. And once we recognize our own sinfulness, we weep. We see that the evil is not somewhere outside us. It is inside us. We ourselves have been complicit with evil.

Secular commentators are becoming increasingly more troubled about trends in America. One of these commentators, syndicated columnist Richard Reeves, once wrote:

> Is America going crazy or is it just me?
>
> I can barely stomach the newspapers here in my hometown. In the tabloids, day after day, the first four or five pages are routinely filled with stories of parents beating or starving their children to death, of children plotting to kill their parents, of people being killed by random gunshots, of people chopping up other people, of cyanide being put in yogurt at the supermarkets. . . .

America, I think, is out of control in some very weird ways. I don't know how bad it really is or exactly why it is happening.

There are obviously many, many reasons, beginning with the unrelenting pressure of living in an open and competitive society. . . . I don't know the answer to any of this. I suspect that things will get worse before they get better.[1]

The author of those words is not, to my knowledge, a Christian. These are the words of a secular commentator, expressing his impression of a secular society that has rejected the wisdom of God. He is trying to make sense of a senseless cultural landscape. He doesn't know how to explain it. The world he lives in sickens him—he can barely stomach the daily news. He can't explain why people do such horrible things to one another. The only thing he seems to know for sure is that these trends will probably grow worse. Writing from a secular perspective, he unwittingly echoes the Word of God.

The Bible tells us that when people and nations turn their back on God and His wisdom, they grow steadily more evil and depraved. We see the proof of this principle splashed across our news media on a daily basis. It makes us weep. It makes us tremble for our children and grandchildren. It makes us fear that they will be victims—or worse, participants—of the corrosive evil of this dying culture.

God gave His Word to us not only to guide us and correct us but also to awaken an awareness that His moral and spiritual laws exist, and they govern our lives. We can no more ignore His moral and spiritual laws than we can ignore His physical laws, such as the law of gravity. Defy His laws at your own peril.

The people who listened to Ezra reading the Word of God before the Water Gate wept because they realized for the first time that they had been living in disregard for God's law—and their entire society had paid a horrible price. So Nehemiah and Ezra comforted the people and put their grief into its proper perspective:

Nehemiah said, "Go and enjoy choice food and sweet drinks, and send some to those who have nothing prepared. This day is holy to our Lord. Do not grieve, for the joy of the LORD is your strength."

The Levites calmed all the people, saying, "Be still, for this is a holy day. Do not grieve."

Then all the people went away to eat and drink, to send portions of food and to celebrate with great joy, because they now understood the words that had been made known to them. (Nehemiah 8:10–12)

When people understand the Word of God, it brings great joy—and, as Nehemiah tells the people, "The joy of the LORD is your strength" (8:10). What a great comfort this is for people who grieve over their own sin and brokenness. The Word of God does not bring condemnation; it brings a message of hope, restoration, and forgiveness. That's why Jesus said, "Blessed are those who mourn, for they will be comforted" (Matthew 5:4).

We will never know what it means to truly be comforted until we learn to mourn. When we see the true awfulness of sin and we grieve over it in the depths of our souls, then we are ready to receive the comfort, strength, and joy of forgiveness.

What does Nehemiah mean by this phrase, "the joy of the LORD"? This joy comes from the amazing fact that God has found a solution to the problem of sin. He has found a way to rebuild our broken lives. By immersing our thoughts in His thoughts, we learn to think as He thinks. We begin to see the world from His point of view. In order to truly hear the thoughts of God, we need to stop listening to the clamoring, babbling voices of the surrounding culture. We need to stop absorbing the philosophy of this dying world and start listening to the words of life contained in the Book of God.

The words of Scripture will mend all the broken places in your life. "He sent out his word and healed them," wrote the psalmist. "He rescued them from the grave" (Psalm 107:20). The ministry of the Word of God is a healing and life-giving ministry. It brings wholeness to our lives and to the lives of those with whom we share the good news.

Hidden Riches Revealed

When God's Word truly seeps into our hearts and affects our lives, something beautiful happens: We become people of godly love and compassion. Nehemiah urged the people, "Go and enjoy choice food and sweet drinks, and send some to those who have nothing prepared" (8:10). The spirit of sharing always floods the souls of those who drink deeply from God's Word.

Next we see that God has anticipated the need of these people. Centuries before, God had provided a visual aid that would remind them of the truth they needed to remember in order to protect their city from any future judgment and destruction:

> On the second day of the month, the heads of all the families, along with the priests and the Levites, gathered around Ezra the teacher to give attention to the words of the Law. They found written in the Law, which the LORD had commanded through Moses, that the Israelites were to live in temporary shelters during the festival of the seventh month and that they should proclaim this word and spread it throughout their towns and in Jerusalem: "Go out into the hill country and bring back branches from olive and wild olive trees, and from myrtles, palms and shade trees, to make temporary shelters"—as it is written.
>
> So the people went out and brought back branches and built themselves temporary shelters on their own roofs, in their courtyards, in the courts of the house of God and in the square by the Water Gate and the one by the Gate of Ephraim. The whole company that had returned from exile built temporary shelters and lived in them. From the days of Joshua son of Nun until that day, the

Israelites had not celebrated it like this. And their joy was very great. (Nehemiah 8:13–17)

Nehemiah is describing the Feast of Tabernacles, a commemoration of the historical event when God called his people out of Egypt. Their departure from Egypt was sudden and hasty. They had no time to sit and eat the Passover meal—they had to eat it standing, dressed in their traveling clothes, with their staffs in hand, ready to move. All the Israelites left Egypt in a single night. After their first day of travel, when they were out in the desert, where did they find shelter? God had told Moses to direct the people to collect tree limbs to build temporary booths for shelter.

God instructed the Israelites to commemorate this event every year. Even though succeeding generations of Israelites had homes in which to dwell, they were to celebrate the Feast of Tabernacles by building temporary booths ("tabernacles") in which to live for seven days. This was to teach the Israelites that they should always see themselves as pilgrims and strangers on the earth. This world was not their home. True blessings were not to be found in this present age but in the glorious age to come.

God wants us to view our lives in the same way. We should not be distressed if we do not acquire all the worldly goods we would like to have. We should not feel let down if we do not achieve our goals and ambitions. We are pilgrims and strangers, and God himself should be our one goal, our only ambition.

That is the message of the Feast of Tabernacles, and it is the truth that will deliver us from the social pressures, envy, and covetousness of our times. We should hold all of our possessions lightly, not clutching them to ourselves. From God's perspective our houses, cars, and bank accounts are of very little importance. If our priorities are right, we can lack all of these things, yet the great treasures of our lives remain untouched.

The worldlings—those who live their lives according to the values of this dying age—spend their lives chasing after worldly possessions. But we as citizens of heaven must remember that we are in the world but not of it. We should never settle for the things others strive for in vain. As C. S. Lewis so wisely said, "Our Father refreshes us on the journey with some pleasant inns, but will not encourage us to mistake them for home."[2]

In our fallenness, we are prone to spiritual amnesia. We easily forget that our true home is in heaven, not here on this dying earth. Yet God has provided a way to help us remember who we truly are and where we truly belong for all eternity. He has provided His Word: "Day after day, from the first day to the last, Ezra read from the Book of the Law of God. They celebrated the festival for seven days, and on the eighth day, in accordance with the regulation, there was an assembly" (v. 18).

Every day, Ezra read the Scriptures to the people. In those days, when the Scriptures were copied by hand and very few people were literate, God's Word had to be read to the people. They could not read it for themselves. So Ezra read the Scriptures day by day, and the people immersed themselves in the thoughts of God.

Realism comes from understanding God's thoughts. When you think as God thinks, you are thinking realistically. You see yourself as you really are, and you see the world as it really is. Godly realism enables you to divest yourself of the illusions and delusions of a confused world. Only when you think realistically can you move toward wholeness, healing, and strengthening of the things that abide.

A number of years ago, I was asked to write an essay called "What the Bible Means to Me." Here is an excerpt from that essay:

> The truth is not always easy for us to hear. Sometimes it pierces me and convicts me. Sometimes I wish I could evade it, and then I am

reminded that it was sent to heal me. Often it encourages me and enheartens me. Sometimes it restores me when nothing else can do so. It confronts me with paradoxes of revelation that intrigue me and challenge me. It exposes the secular illusions of the day and reveals the destructive ends to which they lead. It deals honestly with uncomfortable concepts and opposes the strangleholds of tradition, correcting them with the authority of God.

I have learned to appreciate the Bible most because it brings me face-to-face with my God! Or at least the relationship is so real and personal that it seems to be a face-to-face encounter. My heavenly Father becomes more real and close than any earthly father. I can all but see my Lord and Savior standing beside me and talking to me as I read his words in the gospels. Sometimes the words of Scripture become so vivid and luminous that I feel like kneeling or even falling on my face before the majesty of God. No other book has such power to transport me beyond earth to heavenly places.[3]

This world cares about wealth, power, pleasure, and fame. God's Word contains riches of a different kind—the riches of God's wisdom, the riches of eternal life, and above all, the riches of knowing God himself. These riches are hidden from the eyes of the world, and they are waiting for you and me to discover in His Word. Like the people of Israel in the days of Ezra and Nehemiah, rediscover the hidden riches of God's Word.

Open your Bible, today and every day, and rediscover the riches God has hidden in its pages.

8

††††††††††††††††

HOW TO TALK TO GOD

Nehemiah 9:1–37

Dwight L. Moody (1837–1899) was a great American evangelist and the founder of the Moody Church and Moody Bible Institute in Chicago. As pastor at the Moody Church, he once asked a Christian brother to pray during a worship service. The man rose to his feet, turned his face toward heaven, and began to pray. And pray. And pray. Ten minutes later, he was still praying—and Mr. Moody and his congregation were growing restless.

Finally, Mr. Moody stood up and announced, "While our dear brother continues his prayer, let's turn to hymn number 342 and sing together!"

So, while God never tires of hearing us pray, people sometimes do.

By contrast, there is the story of Bobby Richardson, an outspoken Christian and former New York Yankees second baseman. He once offered a prayer at a Fellowship of Christian Athletes meeting, and that prayer managed to be both amazingly brief and quite profound: "Dear Lord—your will, nothing more, nothing less, nothing else. Amen."

So, when it comes to prayer, that's the long and the short of it.

Here in Nehemiah 9, Nehemiah records the longest prayer in the entire Bible. If long-winded prayers (and long-winded book chapters) make you nervous, don't worry. We will keep this discussion to a reasonable length—and I think you'll find that the prayer Nehemiah records for us here is a great model of prayer that will teach us several profound lessons in how to have a meaningful conversation with God.

Flying Off the Cliff

This prayer is a community event that takes place following the celebration of the Feast of Tabernacles. This was the first time in many years that the Feast of Tabernacles had been observed in Israel. Once the walls of Jerusalem were rebuilt and the gates were reset, and order and prosperity were returning to the city, it was time to celebrate the restoration of the Jewish nation, the Jewish culture, and the Jewish faith. Nehemiah 9 records:

> On the twenty-fourth day of the same month, the Israelites gathered together, fasting and wearing sackcloth and putting dust on their heads. Those of Israelite descent had separated themselves from all foreigners. They stood in their places and confessed their sins and the sins of their ancestors. (vv. 1–2)

While the Feast of Tabernacles had been a time of celebration of God's goodness, the occasion of this prayer was a time of sober self-judgment. It was a time when the people expressed their feelings of grief over their sins. They expressed their grief by refraining from eating and by wearing sackcloth (a crude, rough cloth that we would call burlap). They placed ashes on their heads to outwardly symbolize their inward desolation. They confessed their sins and the sins of their families. They were aware that the sinful practices of one generation are often passed along to the next. We easily forget that this principle still applies today and that we often have to break generational habits and free ourselves from the destructive notions and sinful practices of the past.

What has caused this sudden change of heart among the Israelites? The answer is given to us at the end of this prayer. Let's look ahead and see what has caused these Israelites to mourn, fast, and confess their sins. Speaking to God, they say:

> "But see, we are slaves today, slaves in the land you gave our ancestors so they could eat its fruit and the other good things it produces. Because of our sins, its abundant harvest goes to the kings you have placed over us. They rule over our bodies and our cattle as they please. We are in great distress." (vv. 36–37)

The people who offered this prayer and the people who heard it understood clearly why they had fallen into captivity and slavery. They understood that this was no accident of history. The people of Israel had brought this judgment upon themselves by their sin and rebellion against God.

We are living in similar conditions today—and we don't even seem to realize it. Today's secular "prophets" are troubled by the decline of American culture—but they don't understand that our godlessness and sinfulness is at the root of our rush to self-destruction. One cultural observer, David Walker, was comptroller general of the United States (the government's top accountant), and he warns that America is on the brink of collapse. He writes:

> Many of us think that a super-powerful, prosperous nation like America will be a permanent fixture dominating the world scene.

We are too big to fail. But you don't have to delve far into the history books to see what has happened to other once-dominant powers. . . .

America presents unsettling parallels with the disintegration of Rome—a decline of moral values, a loss of political civility, an overextended military, an inability to control national borders, and the growth of fiscal irresponsibility by the central government. Do these sound familiar?[1]

Many of the symptoms of cultural decline that this man describes—moral decay, political incivility, fiscal irresponsibility, and spiraling debt—can be traced directly to an increasing appetite for greed and sin, along with a growing disregard for God and His laws. Another cultural observer, Niall Ferguson, notes that when civilizations die, they do not slowly wither away. The death of an empire usually occurs with terrifying suddenness. The Roman Empire had stood for five hundred years, yet it collapsed, Ferguson said, "within the span of a single generation." Civilizations can appear to be quite healthy for "some unknowable period," he writes, "then, quite abruptly, they collapse. . . . The shift . . . to destruction and then to desolation is not cyclical. It is sudden."[2]

Our increasingly godless, hedonistic, self-centered civilization reminds me of that cartoon coyote who runs off the edge of a cliff, screeches to a halt in thin air, and realizes he is about to fall to his doom. For the moment, our civilization is still hanging in mid-air—but we have already sailed off the cliff, and our doom awaits us below.

The people of Israel, after spending decades in captivity and slavery in Babylon, knew why their civilization had fallen. They knew why they had been taken into foreign captivity. They knew they had sinned and had forgotten God. The men, women, and children of the nation had all paid the price.

We are fooling ourselves if we think there won't be a price to pay for the sin and godlessness of our culture. We are fooling ourselves if we think our children and grandchildren won't pay the awful price for our sins. We have unparalleled wealth, food, entertainment media, luxuries, cars, smart phones, and computers. Yet because of our sin and our denial of God, all of our material and cultural blessings could disappear overnight.

It happened in ancient Rome. It happened in ancient Israel. And it could happen again, in our own land, our own civilization.

Remembering History in Prayer

Our civilization is not doomed—not yet. We can still come back from the brink of the cliff. We can still come to our senses and come back to God.

In the prayer the Levites pray in Nehemiah 9, we learn how to avoid committing cultural suicide. This prayer was prayed by and on behalf of God's people, Israel. And we, as God's people, the church, can learn from this prayer how to restore our civilization to life and sanity.

The opening verses tell us that the people gathered before God to pray. They fasted and they wept. They pleaded for mercy. And here is an important point: they kept this matter strictly within the family of Israel. They did not involve foreigners. They did not blame others for their plight. They looked to themselves, and they confessed their own sins and the sins of their ancestors.

And there is one more thing they did: "They stood where they were and read from the Book of the Law of the Lord their God for a quarter of the day, and spent another quarter in confession and in worshiping the Lord their God" (v. 3).

The Israelites reckoned a day to be twelve hours long. So the people spent three hours listening as the Book of the Law was read to them. Then they spent three hours confessing their sins and praising God. Later in this passage, we will see that the Levites divided themselves into two groups. Some stood on the stairs leading up to the Water Gate. Others were on a platform on the opposite side of the square. These two groups would call back and forth to the people, one group confessing the sins of the people, the other praising God. Nehemiah writes:

> Standing on the stairs of the Levites were Jeshua, Bani, Kadmiel, Shebaniah, Bunni, Sherebiah, Bani and Kenani. They cried out with loud voices to the LORD their God. And the Levites—Jeshua, Kadmiel, Bani, Hashabneiah, Sherebiah, Hodiah, Shebaniah and Pethahiah—said: "Stand up and praise the LORD your God, who is from everlasting to everlasting." (vv. 4–5)

The first group was the group that led the confession. The second group was the group that led praise. The two groups, then, formed a kind of antiphonal chorus: one group calling out the confession of sin, the other group answering and extolling the glory and mercy of God. The rest of the chapter relates to us the actual prayer they prayed. In this text, we see how to confess sin before God and how to praise Him for His mercy and grace.

First, the people praise God as the creator and maker of all things:

> "Blessed be your glorious name, and may it be exalted above all blessing and praise. You alone are the LORD. You made the heavens, even the highest heavens, and all their starry host, the earth and all that is on it, the seas and all that is in them. You give life to everything, and the multitudes of heaven worship you." (vv. 5–6)

When praising God, this is a great place to begin. Acknowledge the glory of God, who is the maker of all things and the giver of life. We easily forget that every moment of our lives is lived in dependence upon God. We are privileged to draw our next breath and consume our next meal because God himself has sovereignly willed it. If we follow this example of grateful, worshipful prayer, we will never forget all that we owe to our gracious and loving Maker.

We did not create ourselves. We did not fashion the intricate machinery that sustains our bodies—our respiratory and circulatory and neurological system. We seldom stop to think of all the amazing life-giving processes that are taking place every moment at the cellular level of our bodies—processes that sustain our lives day after day. Our hearts beat, our lungs expand and contract—all without conscious effort on our part.

The diaphragm keeps us breathing in and out. Wouldn't it be terrible if we had to lie awake all night, focusing on our breathing, telling ourselves, "Now *dia*, now *phragm*, now *dia*, now *phragm*!" Let us never forget that every breath we take comes from God.

Next, this prayer gives praise to God as the One who calls us and chooses us as His own. He gives undeserved blessings to those He chooses. Nehemiah writes:

> "You are the LORD God, who chose Abram and brought him out of Ur of the Chaldeans and named him Abraham. You found his heart faithful to you, and you made a covenant with him to give to his descendants the land of the Canaanites, Hittites, Amorites, Perizzites, Jebusites and Girgashites. You have kept your promise because you are righteous." (vv. 7–8)

We, who are dead in our sins, are incapable of choosing God. It is God who chooses us. He initiates the call. He awakens in us feelings and desires to draw near to Him. We would never seek God if He had not sought us first. These eternal questions and longings that throb in our minds are planted there by the Spirit of God. Jesus said, "No one can come to me unless the Father who sent me draws them" (John 6:44).

Next, they pray a prayer of thanksgiving and praise to God as the One who delivers from sin and slavery:

"You saw the suffering of our ancestors in Egypt; you heard their cry at the Red Sea. You sent signs and wonders against Pharaoh, against all his officials and all the people of his land, for you knew how arrogantly the Egyptians treated them. You made a name for yourself, which remains to this day. You divided the sea before them, so that they passed through it on dry ground, but you hurled their pursuers into the depths, like a stone into mighty waters. By day you led them with a pillar of cloud, and by night with a pillar of fire to give them light on the way they were to take." (Nehemiah 9:9–12)

This portion of the prayer retells the history of the nation of Israel, beginning with the call of Abraham and continuing with the story of how God, through Moses, delivered the nation from slavery in Egypt. We sometimes treat history with indifference. We forget the words of the Spanish philosopher George Santayana, "Those who cannot remember the past are condemned to repeat it." If we forget the lessons God has taught us through the history of Israel, we will repeat that tragic history. We will plunge our children, our grandchildren, and ourselves into rebellion and slavery.

Those who turn their backs on God end up enslaved—and that enslavement can take many forms. And those who turn back to God find liberation—and that liberation too can take many forms. I heard about a man who found liberation from enslavement to alcohol when he came to Christ—yet he found himself mocked by his old drinking buddies because of his newfound faith in Christ. They said, "Do you believe all those miracles in the Bible?" He replied, "Yes, I do." They said, "Even the one about Jesus changing water into wine?" He said, "Yes, I believe that too." They said, "How did He do it?" The man replied, "I don't know how, but I believe He did it, because in our house, He changed beer into furniture."

When God changes a human heart, the result is deliverance and liberation. That's why, in this prayer, the Israelites praise God for His deliverance of the nation of Israel.

Next, they praise Him as the great Provider of wisdom and the necessities of life:

"You came down on Mount Sinai; you spoke to them from heaven. You gave them regulations and laws that are just and right, and decrees and commands that are good. You made known to them your holy Sabbath and gave them commands, decrees and laws through your servant Moses. In their hunger you gave them bread from heaven and in their thirst you brought them water from the rock; you told them to go in and take possession of the land you had sworn with uplifted hand to give them." (vv. 13–15)

Here we see God's providential care for His own. He taught the Israelites how to live holy lives even though surrounded by great wickedness. He knew He was sending them into a land inhabited by tribes that were morally corrupt. The surrounding tribes openly indulged in vile practices, including offering their children—their own precious children!—to the demon-god Molech. They would throw their children alive into a fiery furnace. No wonder God commanded the Israelites to destroy those tribes and drive them out of the land.

Even when the Israelites failed to remove those tribes from the Promised Land, God commanded them to avoid the moral and spiritual contamination of their pagan practices. He taught the Israelites how to live in the midst of these pagan people without adopting their soul-destroying immorality and false religion.

Today we live in a similar situation. God calls us to live out our faith in the midst of a pagan and post-Christian culture. God has revealed to us in His Word all we need to know about a spiritually, morally, and emotionally healthy way of life. To follow God's prescription for living is true wisdom. To neglect it is self-destructive folly.

God also supplied the needs of the Israelites. He gave them bread to eat when there was no food. He gave them water from a rock in the barren midst of the desert. He met their physical needs—and He met their spiritual needs as well. The New Testament tells us that God's provision for the Israelites in the wilderness is a picture of Christ. Jesus is the Bread of Life and the source of Living Water. As the Israelites learned the meaning of these symbols, they realized that they pointed to the One who was to come, the Anointed One who would meet every need of the human heart—Jesus the Messiah.

The True Character of God

Remember, this prayer is in the form of a two-part antiphonal chorus: one group extols the glory and mercy of God while the other group calls out the confession of sin. At this point in the prayer, the confessing group takes up the theme. In the remainder of Nehemiah 9, we will see an alternation between confession and praise. One group cries out, confessing sin, and the other answers with praise to God:

> "But they, our ancestors, became arrogant and stiff-necked, and they did not obey your commands. They refused to listen and failed to remember the miracles you performed among them. They became stiff-necked and in their rebellion appointed a leader in order to return to their slavery." (vv. 16–17)

This is the course rebellion always follows. When you rebel against God, you invariably return to the evil that once enslaved you. That's what Israel did. They actually wanted to go back to Egypt—back to the beatings and oppression under the heavy hand of Pharaoh. They wanted to go back to the slavery of making bricks without straw. Rebellion is deceptive, and it casts a cloud of spiritual amnesia over the human mind.

After this confession of sin, however, the praise chorus responds. The chorus of praise covers the history of Israel in three divisions. The first division involves the scene at the foot of Mount Sinai:

> "But you are a forgiving God, gracious and compassionate, slow to anger and abounding in love. Therefore you did not desert them, even when they cast for themselves an image of a calf and said, 'This is your god, who brought you up out of Egypt,' or when they committed awful blasphemies." (vv. 17–18)

At this point, I need to digress for a moment and talk about a great American leader, one of our Founding Fathers—Thomas Jefferson. I both admire Jefferson and feel deeply sorry for him. His brilliance in crafting the lofty ideals of the Declaration of Independence was nothing short of miraculous: "We hold these truths to be self-evident, that all men are created equal, that they are endowed by their Creator with certain unalienable Rights . . ."

I pity him because, late in life, his view of the character of God became poisoned by worldly thinking. In a letter to a friend, written in 1820, Jefferson described the God of the Old Testament as "a being of terrific character, cruel, vindictive, capricious and unjust."[3]

Where did Jefferson derive this notion of God as a cruel and vindictive God? Why do so many secularists, atheists, and agnostics today peddle this slander against our loving, merciful God? Throughout the Old Testament, God is described as compassionate, faithful, and patient. He is slow to anger and rich in mercy, and He is eager for His children to return to Him so He can bless them.

Even when the Israelites blasphemed God by creating a golden calf and worshiping it as a god, He spared them and showed mercy to them.

Next, this prayer moves out to the desert and speaks of the years of wandering:

"Because of your great compassion you did not abandon them in the wilderness. By day the pillar of cloud did not fail to guide them on their path, nor the pillar of fire by night to shine on the way they were to take. You gave your good Spirit to instruct them. You did not withhold your manna from their mouths, and you gave them water for their thirst. For forty years you sustained them in the wilderness; they lacked nothing, their clothes did not wear out nor did their feet become swollen." (vv. 19–21)

When was the last time you looked back over your life and counted up the ways God has demonstrated His providential love for you? We tend to take God's blessings for granted. We are far more focused on what we don't have than what we do have. We have bought into the fear that we are missing out, the fear that we don't have enough stuff, the narcissistic notion that we deserve a 5,000-square-foot home with a Mercedes and a Jaguar in the driveway.

But that is not a biblical view of life. That is not God's perspective. He doesn't want us to put our trust in material things. He wants us to put our trust in Him alone. We don't deserve wealth or luxury. We are sinners who deserve only eternal punishment. It is only by the grace of God that He withholds the judgment we truly deserve and showers us with blessings far beyond our deserving. He is compassionate, merciful, and loving. That is what the people of Israel reminded themselves of in this prayer.

Next, there is another chorus of praise to God, focused on the history of Israel in the land of Canaan, and the conquests and achievements that were accomplished by God's hand:

"You gave them kingdoms and nations, allotting to them even the remotest frontiers. They took over the country of Sihon king of Heshbon and the country of Og king of Bashan. You made their children as numerous as the stars in the sky, and you brought them into the land that you told their parents to enter and possess. Their children went in and took possession of the land. You subdued before them the Canaanites, who lived in the land; you gave the Canaanites into their hands, along with their kings and the peoples of the land, to deal with them as they pleased. They captured fortified cities and fertile land; they took possession of houses filled with all kinds of good things, wells already dug, vineyards, olive groves and fruit trees in abundance. They ate to the full and were well-nourished; they reveled in your great goodness." (vv. 22–25)

The people of Israel had spent four centuries as slaves in Egypt. They had never been trained in the art of warfare. They were not an aggressive people. They confronted a land that was populated with cruel, warlike pagan tribes steeped in violence. Yet the Israelites swept into the land of Canaan, conquered the walled fortresses of the Canaanites, and won the land. These events are described in the book of Joshua. The people of Israel recognized God's hand in all of this, and they praised Him for His greatness and His goodness toward them.

Have you thanked God for the victories He has achieved in your life? Have you thanked Him for the promotions you didn't expect to get? For the blessings you didn't deserve? For the consequences and punishment you should have received that God spared you from? I urge you to give God thanks and glory for His hand in your life.

Next, we hear a chorus of confession:

"But they were disobedient and rebelled against you; they turned their backs on your law. They killed your prophets, who had warned them in order to turn them back to you; they committed awful blasphemies. So you delivered them into the hands of their enemies, who oppressed them. But when they were oppressed they cried out to you. From heaven you heard them, and in your great compassion you gave them deliverers, who rescued them from the hand of their enemies.

"But as soon as they were at rest, they again did what was evil in your sight. Then you abandoned them to the hand of their enemies so that they ruled over them. And when they cried out to you again, you heard from heaven, and in your compassion you delivered them time after time." (vv. 26–28)

After God had blessed His people and given them so much, what did they do? They rebelled against Him. They turned their backs on His law. They turned to murder, religious perversion, and sexual perversion. So what choice did God have but to hand them over to the consequences of their sin—not out of anger or hate, but because He loves them too much to allow them to continue in their sin.

Here, the prayer recounts the story of the book of Judges—when Israel came under the domination of alien nations for decades at a time. During their time of oppression, the people would cry out to God, and He would send them a deliverer, a judge. The judges would lead Israel back to the path of righteousness and true worship—for a while. Then the cycle would begin all over again. With each cycle of apostasy, the sins and crimes of the people became worse and worse.

God delivered Israel again and again and again. Here in this prayer we see a marvelous picture of the loving patience of God. He permits us the freedom to go our own way and to taste the results of our own sin. God does not have to punish us directly. Sin itself is punishment. It produces its own consequences. God gets our attention by allowing us to experience the natural consequences of our actions. When we have inflicted enough suffering on ourselves and we call out to God for mercy, He stands ready to deliver us.

A number of years ago, our church took a bold step and invited the president of the Gay People's Union of Stanford University to speak to our young people on the subject: "What the Bible Says about Homosexuality." He came and spoke to us on a Sunday evening, and we gave him plenty of time to make the case that the Bible endorses homosexuality as an alternative lifestyle. We didn't impose any restrictions—he was free to say whatever he liked and to bring literature that promoted his views.

As president of the debating club at Stanford, he was well trained as a speaker and a polemicist. Yet he struggled to make a convincing case. He would read passages from the Bible and attempt to persuade the audience that those passages didn't really say what they clearly said. Even though I was opposed to his position, I actually found it painful to see him floundering so badly.

We had agreed not to argue with him or oppose him during his presentation. After he finished, one of our pastors, Steve Zeisler, gave the biblical perspective. I remember how graciously Steve opened the Scriptures and showed that when God forbids certain practices, it's not because He wants to limit us or oppress us. It's because He wants to protect us from behavior that will hurt us and ruin our lives. Steve showed us from Scripture that homosexuality damages human beings and draws them into a cycle of misery, loneliness, and death.

It was an important event in the ministry of our church, and it opened up a dialogue between our church and people in our community who struggled with homosexual tendencies. We have seen many people delivered by the mercy and power of God. That is what this prayer in Nehemiah 9 expresses. The tough love of God will not willingly let us ruin our lives, but it will always seek to warn us, lovingly confront our sin, and draw us back to himself.

Confessing Our Sins, Not Our Ifs

Next, we see another antiphonal exchange of confession and praise:

"You warned them in order to turn them back to your law, but they became arrogant and disobeyed your commands. They sinned against your ordinances, of which you said, 'The person who obeys them will live by them.' Stubbornly they turned their backs on you, became stiff-necked and refused to listen. For many years you were patient with them. By your Spirit you warned them through your prophets. Yet they paid no attention, so you gave them into the hands of the neighboring peoples. But in your great mercy you did not put an end to them or abandon them, for you are a gracious and merciful God." (vv. 29–31)

Once again, the people confess through prayer the sins of a previous generation. They see clearly that the suffering and captivity they have just emerged from is a direct result of the sins of their ancestors.

Then comes the counterpoint of praise to God for His patience, for warning the people through the prophets, and for being merciful and gracious to His people. God allowed Israel to be subjugated by the Syrians, the Assyrians, and the Babylonians—and His goal was to awaken them to the harm they were inflicting on themselves by their sin and rebellion.

Finally, this prayer moves from past history to present reality. Those who offer this prayer change the pronouns from "they" to "we." The people begin to confess the sins not of the past, but of their own generation:

"Now therefore, our God, the great God, mighty and awesome, who keeps his covenant of love, do not let all this hardship seem trifling in your eyes—the hardship that has come on us, on our kings and leaders, on our priests and prophets, on our ancestors and all your people, from the days of the kings of Assyria until today. In all that has happened to us, you have remained righteous; you have acted faithfully, while we acted wickedly. Our kings, our leaders, our priests and our ancestors did not follow your law; they did not pay attention to your commands or the statutes you warned them to keep. Even while they were in their kingdom, enjoying your great goodness to them in the spacious and fertile land you gave them, they did not serve you or turn from their evil ways.

"But see, we are slaves today, slaves in the land you gave our ancestors so they could eat its fruit and the other good things it produces. Because of our sins, its abundant harvest goes to the kings you have placed over us. They rule over our bodies and our cattle as they please. We are in great distress." (vv. 32–37)

The people acknowledge that they are slaves in their own land. God gave this land to Israel so the people could enjoy its abundant harvests—yet the people have been repeatedly conquered and oppressed by foreign nations, most recently the Babylonians and Persians. Why? All this has come about because of the sins of the people.

And this is exactly the position we find ourselves in as Christians today. There was a time when Americans could live securely in their homes. They could go to bed at night and leave their doors unlocked. But today we are sometimes afraid to walk our own streets at night.

What is the solution? Well, it begins with a prayer of confession of our sins before God and praise to Him for His compassionate mercy. In this prayer, the Levites of Nehemiah's day teach us how to confess—and how to give praise and thanks to God. Notice how they confess their sins honestly and specifically. They say to God, in effect, "You acted faithfully, we acted unfaithfully. You acted graciously, we acted ungratefully."

Many Christians today are masters of the art of the "non-apology apology"—a statement that has the form of an apology without admitting wrongdoing and without expressing any true contrition or remorse. Some examples of non-apology apologies are, "I'm sorry you feel that way," or, "I'm sorry if you were offended," or even,

"Mistakes were made." There's an old prayer that people sometimes pray as a catchall prayer for forgiveness—but in my view, it's really nothing but a non-apology apology:

> If I have wounded any soul today,
> If I have caused one foot to go astray,
> If I have walked in my own willful way,
> Dear Lord, forgive![4]

God has not called us to confess our "ifs." He has called us to confess our sins. The "if" apology ("I apologize *if* I offended anyone") is not a confession—it's a public relations statement. It's designed to get us off the hook. It's designed to make us look better and feel better without admitting any wrongdoing. Genuine confession involves a humble and abject admission of sin, as we see here in this prayer. No excuses. No attempt to avoid responsibility or condemnation. The only sacrifice God wants from us is a broken spirit and a contrite heart.

Today we stand where the people of Israel stood so many years ago. The same two themes we see in this prayer should be the themes of our lives today: (1) the confession of our sin against God, and (2) our praise and worship to God for His patience and mercy toward us. He waits to receive us and pardon us.

He is a God of mercy and forgiveness.

9

††††††††††††††

THE NEW RESOLVE

Nehemiah 9:38–10:39

On November 11, 1620, as the *Mayflower* was anchored near the northern tip of Cape Cod, members of the Plymouth Colony signed a covenant that came to be known as the Mayflower Compact. With this simple document, less than two hundred words long, they established a government based on majority rule. The men of the colony signed it, signifying their agreement to live by these principles "for the glory of God, and the advancement of the Christian faith."

A little more than a century and a half later, a group of American leaders gathered to sign another document—the Declaration of Independence. It was more than just a statement of grievances against Great Britain and more than a declaration of the existence of the new nation. It was a covenant—a binding mutual promise made by the delegates from the thirteen original United States of America.

It concluded: "And for the support of this Declaration, with a firm reliance on the protection of divine Providence, we mutually pledge to each other our Lives, our Fortunes, and our sacred Honor."

History records that some of the signers of the Declaration did, in fact, give up their lives. Some lost their fortunes in the war for independence. But all of them retained their sacred honor.

In the closing verse of Nehemiah 9, the nation of Israel has gathered together as one to pray a prayer of confession and praise to God. The entire nation has expressed a unanimous brokenness of spirit, a unified heart of contrition. Now, at the end of their prayer, the people of the nation seal their prayer with a pledge, a binding covenant: "In view of all this, we are making a binding agreement, putting it in writing, and our leaders, our Levites and our priests are affixing their seals to it" (Nehemiah 9:38).

The people of Israel have emerged from slavery and captivity in Babylon, and they have come back into their homeland. They have rebuilt the walls and gates of their city. Now they wish to commit themselves to a new way of life. They wish to put away sin and devote themselves to God. And they have put this commitment in writing.

This is a powerful demonstration of the need people feel to solemnify a new direction they wish to take. Like the Mayflower Compact and the Declaration of Independence, this document is followed by a list of the signers of the covenant Israel is making. The people signing this document can be divided into four segments of Jerusalem society.

First, Nehemiah lists himself; he signed the covenant in his official capacity as the governor of the province of Judah, the head of the civil government of Israel at that time (Nehemiah 10:1). Second, Nehemiah lists the names of the twenty-two priests who signed this covenant (Nehemiah 10:1–8). Third, he lists the Levites who signed the covenant (Nehemiah 10:9–13). Fourth, he lists the leaders of the people—the nobleman and lesser leaders of the land (Nehemiah 10:14–27).

In addition to all who signed their names to the covenant, Nehemiah tells us that all the common people of Jerusalem, those who did not actually sign the document but were witnesses to the signing, also played a significant role. Nehemiah writes:

> The rest of the people—priests, Levites, gatekeepers, musicians, temple servants and all who separated themselves from the neighboring peoples for the sake of the Law of God, together with their wives and all their sons and daughters who are able to understand—all these now join their fellow Israelites the nobles, and bind themselves with a curse and an oath to follow the Law of God given through Moses the servant of God and to obey carefully all the commands, regulations and decrees of the LORD our Lord. (Nehemiah 10:28–29)

All the people of Jerusalem in the province of Judah bound themselves together into what I call (borrowing a phrase from twentieth-century Quaker scholar Elton Trueblood) "the company of the committed." These were people who decided they would no longer be lukewarm in their religion. Henceforth, they would be radically committed to living out their faith in God by keeping His commandments. They wanted nothing to do with tepid, outward conformity to a cultural religion. Their hearts were on fire for God, and they didn't want their love for God and their zeal for His commandments to ever grow cold.

When human beings have intense feelings about a cause, and they want to commit themselves to it, now and forever, they will pledge themselves to that cause in a binding way. Here, Nehemiah lists six specific commitments these Israelites made to one another and to God: (1) They committed themselves to abstaining from marriage with pagans. (2) They promised to observe the seventh day (the Sabbath), and the seventh year (the Sabbatical). (3) They promised to provide money, grain, and animals for the offerings at the temple. (4) They promised to bring the first fruits of their crops, their herds, their flocks, and their firstborn sons to God. (5) They promised to pay ten percent (the tithe) of all their income, their crops, and their wealth to the temple. (6) They promised to faithfully attend the house of God.

Bigotry—or Wisdom?

Let's look at each of these promises in order, beginning with the promise not to intermarry with unbelievers: "We promise not to give our daughters in marriage to the peoples around us or take their daughters for our sons" (v. 30).

In our melting-pot, multicultural society, this sounds like a bigoted statement. But there was an excellent reason for making that commitment. The idol-worshiping tribes that surrounded Israel engaged in outrageously degenerate religious and sexual practices, including human and infant sacrifice, and the worship of sexual organs, and other degrading practices. Their immorality had spread disease and death among their people.

To protect His people from being contaminated by pagan religion, God had forbidden intermarriage with these pagan cultures. Though intermarriage might seem harmless to us today, we should be careful to avoid the trap of "presentism," imposing our cultural attitudes and norms on cultures of the past without any understanding of the problems those past cultures faced. In order to judge God's prohibition against intermarriage as bigoted, you would have to accept as "normal" some of the gruesome and disgusting practices of the surrounding pagan cultures.

Many secularists and atheists today make this historical error. For example, a prominent popularizer of atheism, Dr. Richard Dawkins, writes in *The God Delusion*, "The God of the Old Testament is . . . a vindictive, bloodthirsty ethnic cleanser" and a "racist . . . bully."[1] Anyone who would make such a statement can only be ignorant of the historical realities of those times. Certainly, Dr. Dawkins would not endorse the practices of those pagan cultures, such as feeding live infants to the furnace of the demon-god Molech.

We don't have to speculate on what would happen if the Israelites violated God's command and intermingled with pagan cultures. We already know, because it happened during the time of the Judges. In fact it happened repeatedly, in cycles. Again and again, when the Israelites intermarried with the pagan tribes around them, the faith, morals, and culture of Israel were corrupted, and the Israelites adopted the degraded practices of their pagan neighbors.

Solomon, David's own son, was said to be the wisest man who ever lived. In his day, polygamy was widely practiced, and Solomon entered into marital relationships with more than a thousand foreign women. The result was that Solomon, who had once been so wise, became an utter fool in his old age. We find his tragic epitaph in the book of 1 Kings:

> King Solomon, however, loved many foreign women besides Pharaoh's daughter—Moabites, Ammonites, Edomites, Sidonians and Hittites. They were from nations about which the LORD had told the Israelites, "You must not intermarry with them, because they will surely turn your hearts after their gods." Nevertheless, Solomon held fast to them in love. He had seven hundred wives of royal birth and three hundred concubines, and his wives led him astray. As Solomon grew old, his wives turned his heart after other gods, and his heart was not fully devoted to the LORD his God, as the heart of David his father had been. He followed Ashtoreth the goddess of the Sidonians, and Molek the detestable god of the Ammonites.

So Solomon did evil in the eyes of the Lord; he did not follow the Lord completely, as David his father had done.

On a hill east of Jerusalem, Solomon built a high place for Chemosh the detestable god of Moab, and for Molek the detestable god of the Ammonites. He did the same for all his foreign wives, who burned incense and offered sacrifices to their gods.

The Lord became angry with Solomon because his heart had turned away from the Lord, the God of Israel, who had appeared to him twice. Although he had forbidden Solomon to follow other gods, Solomon did not keep the Lord's command. (1 Kings 11:1–10)

Solomon and the nation of Israel paid a high price for his folly and disobedience. God does not put these commandments in our way to make us miserable, but to spare us from misery.

The covenantal pledge not to intermarry with pagans was not motivated by bigotry, but by wisdom. The Israelites were hardly a bigoted people. They were all too eager to intermarry with the pagan tribes, always to their undoing. The issue is not race but religion. Any Canaanite, Hittite, Amorite, Perizzite, Jebusite, or Girgashite who converted to faith in the one true God and worshiped according to God's commandments was welcomed into the Israelite community without prejudice.

The Israelites affirmed the principle that the apostle Paul expressed in one of his letters: "Do not be yoked together with unbelievers. For what do righteousness and wickedness have in common? Or what fellowship can light have with darkness?" (2 Corinthians 6:14). This principle is still in force today, and many Christians have violated this principle. They have married someone of a different faith or no faith at all, bringing intense sorrow to themselves, their children, and others.

This doesn't mean that marrying a Christian automatically produces a happy marriage, because there are other biblical principles that also apply. But if you disobey God's command not to be un-equally yoked with unbelievers, you will certainly create enormous heartache and struggle in your marriage—and you may end up like Solomon, departing from the faith.

Is there hope for those who have already violated this principle and married someone outside the faith? Yes. The Bible gives us guidelines for that situation as well (see 1 Corinthians 7 and 1 Peter 3:1). But those who choose a state of being unequally yoked with an unbeliever are choosing to place themselves in a situation that will place their faith in jeopardy. There is no more important basis for life then our faith in God. If you marry someone who doesn't share that foundation for living, what do the two of you truly have in common?

As the Old Testament prophet asks, "Do two walk together un-less they have agreed to do so?" (Amos 3:3). When you choose someone to walk through life with, make sure you both agree on which way you will go.

A Pledge to Keep the Sabbath Day and Sabbatical Year

The second pledge the Israelites made was a promise to keep the seventh day and the seventh year as holy unto the Lord. Nehemiah writes: "When the neighboring peoples bring merchandise or grain to sell on the Sabbath, we will not buy from them on the Sabbath or on any holy day. Every seventh year we will forgo working the land and will cancel all debts" (Nehemiah 10:31).

This is an amazing declaration. God had said, "Six days you shall labor and do all your work, but the seventh day is a sabbath to the LORD your God" (Exodus 20:9–10). What is the seventh day of the week? It is Saturday—not Sunday. Many Christians mistakenly carry the Old Testament restrictions of the Sabbath over into Sunday, the first day of the week. Some even call Sunday "the Sabbath." This is a practice that began quite recently in Christian history, sometime during the nineteenth century.

You may recall the 1981 motion picture *Chariots of Fire*, the biographical film based on the life of Eric Liddell, a Scottish missionary who ran in the 1924 Olympics in Paris. He ran, he said, for the glory of God. When he learned that the hundred-meter race would be on a Sunday—which he considered the Sabbath—he refused to run, in spite of pressure from the British Olympic Committee and the Prince of Wales.

I believe God honored Eric Liddell for his decision, and God used his decision to enlarge his platform for Christian witness. But at the same time, I believe his decision was based on a misunderstanding of Scripture. Sunday is the Lord's Day, and we celebrate it and view it as a day of worship and rest because the Lord Jesus was resurrected on the first day of the week. As Christians, we believe that God wants us to have a day of rest for the body and the soul, and that day is Sunday, the Lord's Day. But Sunday is not the Sabbath.

The Sabbath and the seventh year are both a picture of rest. God teaches us through these symbols that we need rest in the midst of our lives. If we do not pause to rest periodically, we deteriorate mentally and physically. We cannot maintain our mental and physical health by staying constantly active. So a day of rest is a very wise habit to observe.

The day of rest is also God's way of reminding us that we need to learn to rest in God. The Sabbath day, the seventh day, followed the six days of creation. In six days, God created the heavens and the earth, and He rested on the seventh. He stopped creating. He set an example for us, as the book of Hebrews reminds us: "For anyone who enters God's rest also rests from their works, just as God did from his" (Hebrews 4:10).

The Sabbath day is a wonderful visual aid from the Old Testament. What is God teaching us through the Sabbath? He is telling us that we are to work. We are to act. We are to create. We are to make choices and decisions. But we must never forget that all of our activity can never accomplish all that we hope to achieve. Work is good, and God blesses and uses our work for His glory. But we cannot work our way to righteousness or acceptance or eternal life. In order to be righteous, in order to be accepted by God, in order to attain eternal life, we have to rest in God. That is the teaching of the seventh day.

God also wants us to understand that we are to offer our work to God, and let Him bless and use it as He chooses. He can take our inadequate, faltering efforts and turn them into ministry to others and glory for himself. That is the story of the feeding of the five thousand. Jesus took a boy's simple lunch of loaves and fishes, and as He prayed over it and blessed it, God multiplied it to feed five thousand hungry people. That is a picture of our lives if we will rest in the power of God. That too is the teaching of the seventh day.

And what about the seventh year? The teaching of the seventh year encourages us to rest in God's provision and supply. God promises to provide for all of our needs. We see this principle in Leviticus, where the Lord says to Israel:

> "Follow my decrees and be careful to obey my laws, and you will live safely in the land. Then the land will yield its fruit, and you will eat your fill and live there in safety. You may ask, 'What will we eat in the seventh year if we do not plant or harvest our crops?' I will send you such a blessing in the sixth year that the land will yield enough for three years. While you plant during the eighth year, you will eat from the old crop and will continue to eat from it until the harvest of the ninth year comes in." (Leviticus 25:18–22)

The sabbatical year (or *sheviit* in Hebrew) is the seventh year of the seven-year agricultural cycle that God commanded for the land of Israel. It is still observed in Judaism today. During the sabbatical year, the land is left fallow. All agricultural activity, such as planting, pruning, and harvesting, is forbidden. (Only certain practices, such as watering and weeding, which prevent orchards and perennial crops from dying, are allowed.) Any fruit that grows during the sabbatical year is considered ownerless, and it may be picked by anyone. Debts owed by Jews to other Jews are forgiven during the sabbatical year.

This is God's way of teaching His people that we cannot do enough to supply all our needs—but we can trust God to be our Provider. One of the great lessons we see again and again in God's Word is that He will supply all our needs.

As a boy, I was fascinated by a book on the life of missionary Hudson Taylor. He went to China and tossed aside all traditional approaches to reaching the Chinese population. He began to preach and teach, and he discovered amazing lessons about God's ability to supply his needs. He made a statement that became the motto of China Inland Mission (now OMF International): "God's work done in God's way will never lack God's supply."

A number of years ago, I was part of a group of pastors and lay people planning the first Congress on Biblical Exposition (COBE). We needed a huge amount of money, and we had no list of donors who would support the effort. We realized we needed at least $200,000 in cash within a week, or the effort would fail and could not be continued. A group of us gathered at the Mount Hermon Christian Conference Center near Santa Cruz, California, and we set our need before the Lord. We said, "Lord, this is your work. If you want it to succeed, you must supply."

Later that evening, I attended a meeting unrelated to our effort to launch COBE. Our group never mentioned the financial need to anyone at Mount Hermon. Yet, to my astonishment, a man came up to me that evening and gave me a check for $50,000. He told me I should use it wherever the need was greatest.

Later that evening, I heard from several other people who had prayed that day for God's provision. They had unexpectedly received checks, cash, and promises of money to come—and when we totaled these gifts, we realized we had the $200,000 we had prayed for. That was God's supply of our needs. He was teaching us that we didn't need to strive and work and beat the bushes for that money. We can rest in Him, and He will supply.

The secular world believes that wealth comes through planning, hard work, advertising, salesmanship, and other worldly practices. But God says, "I will supply your needs. Rest in me." That is the lesson of the sabbatical year.

A Pledge to Make Offerings

The third pledge the people make is to provide money, grain, and animals as sacrificial offerings at the temple.

> "We assume the responsibility for carrying out the commands to give a third of a shekel each year for the service of the house of our God: for the bread set out on the table; for the regular grain offerings and burnt offerings; for the offerings on the Sabbaths, at the New Moon feasts and at the appointed festivals; for the holy offerings; for sin offerings to make atonement for Israel; and for all the duties of the house of our God.
>
> "We—the priests, the Levites and the people—have cast lots to determine when each of our families is to bring to the house of our God at set times each year a contribution of wood to burn on the altar of the LORD our God, as it is written in the Law." (Nehemiah 10:32–34)

The Israelites realized that in the past they had failed God by disobeying His commandments regarding offerings and sacrifices. So they renewed their pledge to keep this commandment year after year.

The offerings that God had instituted served two purposes. The offering of crops and grain and money served to support the temple as the central institution of Israelite society. And the animal sacrifices placed an emphasis on the shedding of blood, which was God's lesson to the people that the shedding of innocent blood was a requirement for the forgiveness of sin. The animal sacrifices pointed forward in time to the coming of the Messiah and to His crucifixion.

The history of Israel shows that the character of the nation revolved around animal sacrifices and offering up crops and grain to God. Whenever these offerings fell into disuse in Israel, the people forgot their God and forgot the cost of redemption. The blood sacrifices reminded the people that only death can solve the problem of sin. Good works, religious rituals, donating money—none of these things can remove our guilt. Only the blood of Christ makes us clean. That's why Hebrews 9:22 tells us, "the law requires that nearly everything be cleansed with blood, and without the shedding of blood there is no forgiveness."

Unfortunately, we hear very little anymore about the blood of Jesus. Some ministers have begun to soft-pedal or even avoid the subject of the blood of Christ out of fear that their parishioners will be offended. But if the blood of Christ offends us, how can we be saved? We cannot be saved if the very thing that saves us is offensive to us.

In early 1989, a missionary couple in Canada, George and Vera Bajenksi, received a phone call informing them that their son Ben had been gravely injured in an accident near his high school. They got in their car and rushed to the intersection. They found police cars and an ambulance on the scene—and they saw their son's body lying on the pavement in a large pool of blood.

Vera Bajenksi said, "George, Ben went home—home to be with Jesus."

As she later recalled, she wanted to somehow put all that blood back into Ben's body. "That blood," she said, "became the most precious thing in the world because it was life. It belonged in my son, my only son, the one I loved so much."

George Bajenksi recalled the heartbreak of seeing cars driving through Ben's blood on the pavement. He wanted to tell those drivers, "You will not drive over the blood of my son!"

In the midst of their grief, George and Vera Bajenksi discovered an amazing insight. They realized how God the Father must have grieved when His only Son bled and died on the cross. By shedding the blood of His Son on the cross, God spoke to humanity with the strongest, most powerful image He could find. He spoke to us through the language of blood. That is why the blood of Christ is so comforting to believers—and offensive to those who do not believe.[2]

The bloody offerings at the temple prepared the way for the death of Jesus and for the remembrance of His death at the Lord's Table. We ought to meditate on the blood of Jesus every day. We must never forget the cost of our redemption. As the apostle Peter reminds us, "For you know that it was not with perishable things such as silver or gold that you were redeemed from the empty way of life handed down to you from your ancestors, but with the precious blood of Christ, a lamb without blemish or defect" (1 Peter 1:18–19).

The fourth pledge the people made was closely related to the third pledge. It is a promise to commit the firstfruits of their crops, herds, flocks, and even their sons to God.

"We also assume responsibility for bringing to the house of the LORD each year the firstfruits of our crops and of every fruit tree.

"As it is also written in the Law, we will bring the firstborn of our sons and of our cattle, of our herds and of our flocks to the house of our God, to the priests ministering there.

"Moreover, we will bring to the storerooms of the house of our God, to the priests, the first of our ground meal, of our grain offerings, of the fruit of all our trees and of our new wine and olive oil." (Nehemiah 10:35–37)

Why was God so concerned that the first of everything be dedicated to Him? God tells us in His original command in the book of Exodus:

"After the LORD brings you into the land of the Canaanites and gives it to you, as he promised on oath to you and your ancestors, you are to give over to the LORD the first offspring of every womb. All the firstborn males of your livestock belong to the LORD. Redeem with a lamb every firstborn donkey, but if you do not redeem it, break its neck. Redeem every firstborn among your sons.

"In days to come, when your son asks you, 'What does this mean?' say to him, 'With a mighty hand the LORD brought us out of Egypt, out of the land of slavery. When Pharaoh stubbornly refused to let us go, the LORD killed the firstborn of both people and animals in Egypt. This is why I sacrifice to the LORD the first male offspring of every womb and redeem each of my firstborn sons.' And it will be like a sign on your hand and a symbol on your forehead that the LORD brought us out of Egypt with his mighty hand." (Exodus 13:11–16)

Here God calls upon the Israelites to recognize His ownership rights over their lives. He redeemed them out of Egypt—and His redemption of Israel out of slavery prefigured His redemption of the human race out of bondage to sin through the firstborn of God, Jesus Christ.

At Peninsula Bible Church, we believe it is so important to remember God's right of ownership that we have these words from 1 Corinthians 6:19–20 written across the front of our auditorium:

"You are not your own; you are bought at a price." As Christians, we acknowledge that God owns us. We do not own ourselves.

The world says, "You are your own. If you are pregnant and you do not want the baby, you can kill that baby, because you have a total right to do whatever you please with your own body." Never mind what you are doing to the body and life of your baby. Never mind what God says about your body. In our post-Christian culture today, the individual is sovereign, and God has no say over us.

But the Bible tells us that God is sovereign, He owns us, we are not our own, and we don't have the right to do anything we choose with our bodies. God gave us our bodies, God redeemed us, and God paid the price we could never afford. We owe Him all that we are and have, including our bodies.

If Jesus is truly the Lord of our lives, then He—not we—has the right to choose whom we will marry, where we will live, the path our career will take, the church we will attend, and on and on. That was God's message to Israel, and that is His message to you and me. We belong to God. He bought us and He paid for us. We do not own ourselves.

To those who live by the self-centered, rebellious values of this fallen and dying world, being owned by God is the worst fate imaginable. To those of us who have experienced the grace, mercy, and blessings of our loving heavenly Father, God's ownership of us is the most wonderful news we could hear.

Do Not Neglect the House of God

The fifth pledge the people make is a promise to faithfully give a tithe, the tenth part of their wealth. Nehemiah writes:

"And we will bring a tithe of our crops to the Levites, for it is the Levites who collect the tithes in all the towns where we work. A priest descended from Aaron is to accompany the Levites when they receive the tithes, and the Levites are to bring a tenth of the tithes up to the house of our God, to the storerooms of the treasury. The people of Israel, including the Levites, are to bring their contributions of grain, new wine and olive oil to the storerooms, where the articles for the sanctuary and for the ministering priests, the gatekeepers and the musicians are also kept." (Nehemiah 10:37–39)

The prophet Malachi was a contemporary of Nehemiah. Speaking for God, Malachi said to the people:

"Bring the whole tithe into the storehouse, that there may be food in my house. Test me in this," says the LORD Almighty, "and see if I will not throw open the floodgates of heaven and pour out so much blessing that there will not be room enough to store it." (Malachi 3:10)

The pledge to faithfully pay the tithe is the response of the people to Malachi's appeal. God ordained that the tithes would be used to support the temple and the ministry of the Levites and priests. The Old Testament priesthood was ordained to provide spiritual guidance to the people.

Many Christians today still feel bound by the tithe. But in the New Testament, the tithe is no longer laid upon believers as a requirement. The New Testament teaches that Christians are to give a portion of their wealth to the Lord in recognition of all His blessings. Each believer is permitted to determine that portion for himself or herself, as Paul has written: "On the first day of every week, each one of you should set aside a sum of money in keeping with your income" (1 Corinthians 16:2). To explore New Testament principles of giving more thoroughly, read 1 Corinthians 16 and 2 Corinthians 8 and 9.

So God gives us the freedom to choose for ourselves how much we should give to Him. He is not primarily concerned with our money, but with our motive. God looks upon the heart. Offerings mean nothing to God if they do not pour from a cheerful spirit and a thankful heart. Yes, our offerings do support God's ministry, but we need to give those offerings willingly, gratefully, and joyfully.

God has ordained that the ministry of the church should be supported not out of legalistic obligation, but out of gratitude. If God has blessed your life, if you are grateful to Him because of the way He has changed your life, if He has poured out His blessings on you in the good times and He has comforted you in the difficult times, if He has healed your hurts and your brokenness, then your heart should be filled with gratitude. Out of that gratitude comes a desire to give.

Some Christians can only afford to give five percent; I've known others who were able to give ninety-five percent of their wealth and could live on the remaining five percent. If God has blessed you greatly, how can you show your gratitude to Him? This is a question you and only you can answer.

Next, we find the sixth and final pledge the people make to God and each other in the concluding phrase of the chapter: "We will not neglect the house of our God" (Nehemiah 10:39).

The people are absolutely committed to faithfully attending the worship services at the temple. Throughout the history of Israel, the temple has been called "the house of God." He signified His presence in the temple by the Shekinah Glory, which was located in the Holy of Holies.

Today, we live under the New Testament, and we do not call any building "the house of God." If you study the New Testament teachings with care, you see that it never refers to any physical building as "the house of God." Instead, the house of God is made up of people.

During my time in the pastorate, one of our pastors, David Roper, once said that we should not have a sign in front of our church building that says, "Peninsula Bible Church." Instead, the sign in front of our building should read, "Peninsula Bible Church Meets Here." It is the people, not the building, that is the church. It is the people, not the building, that is truly "the house of God." Whether a church meets in a church building, a storefront, a school auditorium, a theater, or a private home, the church is the people, not the building. And wherever God's people meet, God meets with them there.

The church is not a place. The church is a dynamic history-making, life-changing force. The church exists for the purpose of making a difference in the world and in human lives. We need the life-changing ministry of other believers in our lives. The apostle Paul prayed that all believers would come to know "how wide and long and high and deep is the love of Christ, and to know this love that surpasses knowledge" (see Ephesians 3:18–19).

We cannot experience the true width, length, height, and depth of the love of Christ without the ministry of other believers. This is one of the principal reasons God established the church. Not only does the church exist to be a witness to this fallen world of the good news of Jesus Christ but it also exists to be a place of healing and encouragement for all believers. That is why the book of Hebrews tells us, "And let us not neglect our meeting together, as some people do, but encourage one another, especially now that the day of his return is drawing near" Hebrews 10:25 NLT).

I remember a conversation I had with two members of our church, men of very different temperament, background, and economic class. Out in secular society, it is unlikely that these two men would have been acquainted with each other. Yet here in the church, they were working closely in ministry together. They were good friends because of their partnership in ministry, and this affinity was an important blessing in their lives. Through the church, they had learned to appreciate someone different from themselves. They had learned to bridge differences through Christian unity and Christian love.

Had there been struggles in their relationship? Yes, they said they had experienced a number of conflicts—and they had learned to be tolerant and patient toward each other. They had learned that unity in the Spirit does not mean unanimity in all decisions. God had used these disagreements in their relationship to help them to grow more mature in Him. God had even shown them that those who irritate us can often be of great benefit to us, as long as we are committed to loving them, forgiving them, and accepting them for the sake of our Lord.

The people of Jerusalem made a commitment to one another, "We will not neglect the house of our God." In Old Testament times, the house of God was a building—the temple. Today, the house of God is people. We are the house of God. We must not neglect our brothers and sisters in the faith, because we are the house of God.

I wish I could say that the people kept the promises they made that day. But this story has a tragic ending. The Israelites failed to keep their commitments. They allowed the old habits to creep back into their lives. They began walking in their old sins once again—and the nation lost God's blessing.

Why did they fail to keep the promises they made? Why did they go back on their word? I believe the answer can be found in Nehemiah 10:29: "All these now join their fellow Israelites the nobles, and bind themselves with a curse and an oath to follow the Law of God given through Moses the servant of God and to obey carefully all the commands, regulations and decrees of the LORD our Lord."

The people did not rely on the power of God. They relied on their own efforts to obey. They bound themselves with a curse and an oath, which was intended to reinforce their own self-determination, their own willpower. They gritted their teeth and swore to be faithful to this promise—but nowhere did they express a need for help from God in keeping this pledge. Nowhere did they express an expectation that God himself would empower them to do His will.

You see, we have something today, in New Testament times, that these Old Testament people didn't have. We have Christ, and through Him we have the Holy Spirit. It is right to make a pledge to be obedient to God. There is nothing at all wrong with writing down that pledge and signing it as a sign of our commitment to God. But we should always add the words that Paul himself wrote: "For I can do everything through Christ, who gives me strength" (Philippians 4:13 NLT).

Let us pledge ourselves to carrying out God's commandments in the community of faith—and let us rely on Him for the power to keep that pledge. We cannot hope to obey Him and please Him in our own faltering strength. But we can do all things—even this—through Christ who gives us strength.

10

††††††††††††††

THE WAYS GOD WORKS

Nehemiah 11:1—12:26

Stanley Baldwin was prime minister of Great Britain in the 1920s and 1930s. Before becoming prime minister, Baldwin served as financial secretary to the treasury. After the First World War, Baldwin was deeply concerned at the large amount of war debt Great Britain had accumulated. In 1919, the year after the war ended, he wrote a letter that was published in *The Times* of London, urging wealthy Britons to help eliminate the war debt by voluntarily taxing themselves twenty percent of their net worth and donating that amount to the treasury.

Baldwin valued his own holdings at about £580,000, so 20 percent of his net worth was about £116,000. He generously rounded that up to £150,000, liquidated that amount of his personal estate, purchased £150,000 of government war-loan bonds—then he destroyed the certificates so they could never be cashed in. In this way, he made a generous £150,000 gift to the treasury, in addition to the income tax he paid that year.

He was disappointed to learn, however, that few if any of his wealthy countryman followed his example. Though thousands of young men had volunteered to serve Great Britain during the war, Stanley Baldwin found that it was not easy to convince people to sacrifice for their country once the crisis had passed.

As we come to Nehemiah 11, we will find that Nehemiah faces a similar challenge: How will he convince people to volunteer for the good of their nation? At this point in the account, the city wall was rebuilt, and Jerusalem had become a strong and well-defended city—yet it was a city without people. So Nehemiah had to find a way to repopulate Jerusalem.

The leaders of Israel lived in Jerusalem because the city was the seat of the central government. But the city had no commerce, no merchants, no shopkeepers. During the reconstruction of the walls and gates, people had come from the towns and villages around Jerusalem to serve as workers and guards, defending the city from its enemies during the reconstruction project.

But once the project was completed and the crisis was past, most of those workers left the city and returned to their homes and families in the surrounding region. So Jerusalem, which had become a busy and bustling metropolis during the reconstruction phase, was suddenly empty and vulnerable once more. Although the city's walls were stronger than ever, there were far fewer men to guard those walls. Jerusalem had lost many defenders, but it had lost none of its enemies, so the city was still under threat.

Nehemiah knew there was strength in numbers, so the greater the population of Jerusalem the more secure the city would be. More people meant more warriors and more strength in battle—but how could Nehemiah persuade large numbers of people to leave their homes in the countryside and come live in Jerusalem, a city that would be perpetually targeted for destruction by its enemies?

Nehemiah's dilemma—and his solution to that dilemma—will provide some surprisingly practical lessons that we can apply to our lives today.

Voluntarily Drafted

The opening verses of Nehemiah 11 describe Nehemiah's solution to Jerusalem's under-population problem. He is going to "draft" families to Jerusalem, much as governments draft young men into the military:

> Now the leaders of the people settled in Jerusalem. The rest of the people cast lots to bring one out of every ten of them to live in Jerusalem, the holy city, while the remaining nine were to stay in their own towns. The people commended all who volunteered to live in Jerusalem.
>
> These are the provincial leaders who settled in Jerusalem (now some Israelites, priests, Levites, temple servants and descendants of Solomon's servants lived in the towns of Judah, each on their own property in the various towns, while other people from both Judah and Benjamin lived in Jerusalem). (vv. 1–4)

In order to be fair to all, the people cast lots to select one-tenth of the population to be "drafted" to live in Jerusalem. It was a means of selecting people as a random sample from a larger population (a similar system, called *sortition*, is used today to randomly and fairly select jurors from a jury pool). We don't know exactly how the lots were cast. The practice of casting lots might involve the selection of sticks of various lengths or tossing dice or flat stones. The practice of casting lots is mentioned throughout Scripture—seventy times in the Old Testament and seven times in the New Testament.

Evidently, being selected by casting lots did not necessarily mean that a person or family would be forced to move to Jerusalem. Undoubtedly, those who would undergo severe hardship (such as having a family emergency or being unable to make a living) would be excused from having to move to Jerusalem. So those who were chosen by lots and who agreed to go were "volunteers" in every sense of the word, even though they were "drafted" by the casting of lots.

It's important to remember, as we read Old Testament history, that these events are often pictures and symbols that describe how we ought to live in the spiritual realm today. As we view the Old Testament through this lens, many biblical stories become powerful lessons for our lives today.

One of the lessons of Nehemiah 11 is that God is the Builder and we are His city. The New Testament tells us that God is building a city called the New Jerusalem. This new heavenly city is not like the old one, made of bricks and mortar. It is a new city built of spiritual stones—"living stones," as we read in 1 Peter 2:5. The New Jerusalem will be inhabited by all who have been redeemed by grace through faith.

Just as God will one day populate His New Jerusalem, Nehemiah must populate Jerusalem as the capital of the nation. It makes no sense to have a capital city that is uninhabited. So, as governor of Judah, Nehemiah issued an edict, stating that one out of every ten people living in the Greater Jerusalem Area had to move inside the city limits. He went through the towns and numbered the people, counting them off by tens. Then they cast lots to determine which families would be expected to move.

The voluntary nature of this selection is spiritually significant. Although people were chosen by lot to move from the suburbs into the city, they were permitted to decline and to nullify the result of the random selection. Then the lots would be cast again and another name would be chosen. Ultimately, someone who was selected by the casting lots would freely consent to move to Jerusalem. Those who consented to go received honors and accolades from all the people because they had volunteered to do what God called them to do.

It's not hard to apply this aspect of the story to our lives today. The same principle that applied in ancient Israel still applies in the church today. According to the New Testament, we are all called into the ministry—all of us without exception. We tend to think of "ministry" as work done by professional clergy. That's why we call such people "ministers."

But God tells us in His Word that the work of the ministry belongs to all the saints—that is, to all Christians. The moment you receive Jesus Christ as your Lord and Savior, you are a part of God's kingdom. God calls you to take up your labor in His kingdom and to do the work of the ministry according to the spiritual gift He has given you.

But God does not force you into ministry. You must volunteer for ministry. God asks us, and He gives us spiritual gifts—but we are free to refuse God and neglect our spiritual gifts. But if we want to be honored and commended by the saints, and by the Lord himself, then we would be wise to volunteer to perform in the realm of ministry He has opened up for us.

The lots have been cast. We have been selected. God has called us into ministry. Will we accept that call or reject it? All have been drafted, but only a few have voluntarily reported for duty. Make sure that when God calls, you become a volunteer draftee.

Your voluntary ministry in His name will earn you a lasting reward in heaven and the words, "Well done, good and faithful servant," from your Lord and Master.

Lessons from a List of Names

The rest of Nehemiah 11 and the first twenty-six verses of Nehemiah 12, I must confess, read very much like a telephone book. Yet

I have always found this principle, given to us by the apostle Paul, to be true: "All Scripture is God-breathed and is useful for teaching, rebuking, correcting and training in righteousness" (2 Timothy 3:16). Whenever we are reading Scripture and we come upon an apparently dry and uninteresting list of names, it's time to reflect more deeply on what God wants to teach us through that passage. God always includes clues to a deeper meaning. If we follow those clues with care, they will lead us to unexpected insights—and that "telephone book" passage will come alive with meaning for our lives.

Let's look at some of the clues we find here in this passage. I think we're about to make some interesting discoveries. I won't reproduce the entire text here in this chapter, but you may want to keep your Bible open to Nehemiah 11 and 12 as we go along.

Beginning with Nehemiah 11:4, the texts contains two lists of names, some from the tribe of Judah and some from the tribe of Benjamin. These are the two tribes of Israel that made up the Southern Kingdom of Judah. These two tribes were made up of many families that had settled in the region around Jerusalem, and there was mingling and intermarriage between these two tribes. In verses 4 through 9 we see that 468 brave men of Judah and 928 men of Benjamin volunteered to live in Jerusalem.

The names of the descendants of Judah focus on one ancestor whose name is Perez. Verse 6 concludes, "The descendants of Perez who lived in Jerusalem totaled 468 men of standing." Whenever you come across a statement like this in Scripture—a statement that singles out an individual from the past—it's a signal, a hint, that we should take a closer look at the life of that person. Who, then, was Perez, and what is the significance of his name here in Nehemiah 11?

Perez was one of the sons of Judah, who was in turn the son of Jacob, the patriarch who fathered the twelve tribes of Israel. The story of the birth of Perez is found in Genesis 38. It is a sordid story of how Judah conceived his son Perez with his own daughter-in-law, Tamar. This sexual sin resulted in a pregnancy.

When Tamar was in labor, the midwife discovered that Tamar was about to deliver twins. The twin brother of Perez began to emerge first, so the midwife tied a scarlet string around the baby's finger to indicate that he would be the elder twin. However, the baby pulled his arm back in, and the other twin emerged first. Because the second baby broke out of the womb that way, he was named Perez, meaning "breaking out."

Perez's descendants are traced in almost every generation since. Nehemiah lived centuries after Perez, yet Nehemiah makes a point of stating that these brave men of Judah were descended from Perez. Nehemiah makes a point of calling the descendants of Perez who lived in Jerusalem "men of standing" (or, in some translations, "brave men").

No similar phrase is attached to the list of the descendants of Benjamin, even though the relatively small tribe of Benjamin contributed twice as many men as the much larger tribe of Judah. I don't think any insult is meant to the descendants of Benjamin. Rather, the reference to the descendants of Perez as "men of standing" is a mark of distinction for his family.

There is a tragic stain on the history of the tribe of Benjamin found in the last few chapters of the book of Judges. There we read the sorry tale of the men of that tribe who fell into sexual sin and began to practice homosexuality. Despite this disgrace in the family history, two important men emerged from the tribe of Benjamin. Both were named Saul.

One was King Saul, the first king of Israel. Though he started well, he ultimately proved to be a great disappointment. He ended his forty-year reign in bitter, angry rebellion against God. Saul's story ended when he took his own life on the battlefield to avoid being captured by the Philistines (see 1 Samuel 31).

The second Saul is found in the New Testament. He also came from the tribe of Benjamin. He was Saul of Tarsus, better known to us as the apostle Paul. In contrast to the first Saul, Saul of Tarsus began in bitter, angry rebellion against God, but ended his life as a missionary who took the gospel from Palestine across Asia Minor and into Europe. According to tradition, Paul was executed in Rome—where he had been under house arrest and where he had written letters to his churches and preached the gospel.

What is the lesson we learn from the descendants of Perez and the descendants of Benjamin? What do these lists of names teach us? I believe this text in Nehemiah 11 illustrates a truth that is taught throughout the New Testament: God is no respecter of persons. God does not care how you started out in life. Throughout the Scriptures, we see that God can take people out of the most humble and lowly circumstances, and He can use them in a mighty way. He often chooses the obscure person, the once-tainted, the outcast, the rejected person to achieve His purpose in the world.

The lineage of Jesus the Messiah includes four women who fit this description—Tamar, the mother of Perez, who posed as a prostitute in order to sleep with her father-in-law Judah; Rahab, the harlot of Jericho; Ruth, the woman of Moab who was redeemed and married into the family of Boaz; and Bathsheba, the woman with whom King David committed adultery in 2 Samuel 11. God is in the business of redeeming sinners and elevating the lowly. As the apostle Paul wrote, "But God chose the foolish things of the world to shame the wise; God chose the weak things of the world to shame the strong" (1 Corinthians 1:27).

Or, as someone once paraphrased that verse, "God pickles the proud and preserves the foolish." So no one should feel overly proud about being a highborn blueblood—and no one should feel ashamed, unworthy, or set on a shelf by God because of lowly beginnings. You are the you God made you to be, and He will use you greatly if you voluntarily make yourself available to Him.

What Kind of Priest Are You?

Nehemiah 11:10–24 is another lengthy section filled with many names. Again, the temptation is to skip over these names without thinking about them or even glancing at them. Yet these names form a picture of God's provision for ministry within the city of Jerusalem. Once the capital city is populated, it will be filled with problems and hurts and needs.

Wherever you have people, you have people problems. You have people struggling with losses and sorrows. You have people in conflict with one another. You have people who are sick or injured, people who struggle financially, people who are under enormous stress. So the city needed the ministry of individuals who were dedicated and trained to help strengthen the people of the city. Their job was to maintain the spiritual life of Jerusalem.

First, we see the selection of a company of 1,192 priests. There are three groups of priests. First, there were 822 priests who carried on the work of the temple. These were the officiating priests. They offered sacrifices, presented offerings, and performed the rituals Moses had prescribed. They were the ones who ministered to the spiritual life of the people.

Next, there was a second group of 242 priests who were set aside as heads of families. There are a number of views as to what is meant by "heads of families." I believe that these 242 priests had a special ministry to the families of the priests. They were responsible to counsel families and work out the problems and difficulties that are common to family life. I'm sure they were especially attentive to the needs of their own families as they ministered to other priestly families.

Then there was a third group of 128 men who are called "men of standing" in the NIV, but are referred to as "mighty men of valor" in other translations. Clearly, Jerusalem was a city ringed with enemies, and the city needed to be defended by warriors, including warriors of the priestly class. These priests were called upon from time to time to take up their swords and shields and defend their city in battle.

We can find parallels to these three groups of "priests" in the church today. Remember (as we saw when we were exploring Nehemiah 7) that "priests" in the church today are not a separate class from everyone else, but we are all part of the priesthood of all believers. The Lord Jesus is our High Priest, and He has made us all to be a royal priesthood in a priestly kingdom (see 1 Peter 2:9). We are all called to be in ministry, and there are at least three kinds of ministries where we may serve.

First, like the priests who served by leading worship and making sacrifices and offerings in the temple, some of us will be called to use our gifts in leading worship, teaching the people, and helping the people understand the meaning of the great sacrifice of Jesus. Some of us in the church, whether we are pastors or laypeople, have spiritual gifts that enable us to teach the doctrines of redemption and forgiveness of sin, so people can understand how to become a new creature in Christ.

Second, like the priests who served as "heads of families," many among us are especially gifted in helping families resolve problems and crises. Again, you find such gifts among both pastors and laypeople, and every Christian should view himself or herself as having a ministry in the church.

Third, there were priests who were also warriors—and today, there are genuine warriors within the priesthood of all believers in the church. What sort of battles are they engaged in? The most important warfare we face is spiritual warfare. Our struggle is not against flesh and blood, but against spiritual rulers and forces of evil (Ephesians 6:12). So, as priestly warriors, we must put on the full armor of God—the belt of truth, the breastplate of righteousness, the shoes of the gospel, the shield of faith, the helmet of salvation, and the sword of the Spirit, which is God's Word (vv. 14–17). Where do we go to war? On our knees—in prayer.

Also, there is another kind of warrior in the priesthood of all believers. We must go to war against the moral and spiritual deception that darkens the minds of the people around us. Again, your atheist professor, your neighbor in a cult, your hedonist coworker, your homosexual brother-in-law—these people are not your enemy. They are casualties of your enemy. They may be hostile to you, they may hate you and everything you stand for, and they may even persecute you—but as Jesus prayed on the cross (Luke 23:34), let us pray that God would convert them and forgive them, because they really don't know what they're doing. Your real enemy is a malevolent spiritual being called Satan.

The best way to attack lies is to take a stand for the truth. The more you proclaim the truth, the less you have to attack the lies of false religions or philosophies. Speak the truth in love on social media, over coffee with friends, over the backyard fence, at the gym, on the campus, and by the water cooler. Be a gentle, compassionate, gracious warrior for God's truth.

God still works the same way today as He did in Nehemiah's time. All of us in the Lord's congregation are priests. Let us be about our priestly business of strengthening one another in the church and spreading the Good News to the world beyond.

The Ministry of Music

The next group we see, in verses 15 through 18, are the Levites. There were 284 Levites living in the holy city. They are divided into two groups. The first division "had charge of the outside work of the house of God" (see Nehemiah 11:16). What was their ministry? This first group of Levites was comparable to what most New Testament churches would recognize as a group of deacons. These are men and women responsible to care for the buildings and for the material needs of the poor, sick, and elderly.

This second group of Levites was made up of the musicians. If you look at them carefully, you will notice a number of familiar names. There is Mattaniah, the director of thanksgiving and prayer, who is the great-grandson of Asaph. And there is Abda, the grandson of Jeduthun. These two names, Asaph and Jeduthun, appear frequently in the Psalms. Asaph was a psalmist, and Jeduthun was a director of music. They led the congregation of Israel in praise and worship in the time of King David.

In 1 Chronicles 16:41, we read that two men, Heman and Jeduthun, were among those who were "chosen and designated by name to give thanks to the LORD, 'for his love endures forever.'" The steadfast love of God is the central theme of all thanksgiving. The great hymns and praise choruses of the faith are songs of praise to God for His enduring love. That is the theme of John Newton's hymn "Amazing Grace." It is also the theme of another hymn by the nineteenth-century Scottish songwriter George Matheson, a hymn I never tire of hearing:

> O Love that wilt not let me go,
> I rest my weary soul in thee;
> I give thee back the life I owe,
> That in thine ocean depths its flow
> May richer, fuller be.[1]

This second group of Levites conducted a ministry of music. Let's never forget that music in the church is not entertainment—it is ministry. It is a means by which we can be strengthened, built up, and encouraged in our faith.

Many times I have been in the audience of a worship service or Bible conference, and my soul has been blessed and strengthened by the ministry of the musicians, the choir, and the solos. I have been moved to tears of joy and gratitude for everything the Lord has done for me. That is the ministry of music to the human heart.

There is another Old Testament passage that fascinates me: "David, together with the commanders of the army, set apart some of the sons of Asaph, Heman and Jeduthun for the ministry of prophesying, accompanied by harps, lyres and cymbals" (1 Chronicles 25:1). Later in that same chapter, we read that Jeduthun "prophesied, using the harp in thanking and praising the Lord" (1 Chronicles 25:3). And in 2 Chronicles we read:

> All the Levites who were musicians—Asaph, Heman, Jeduthun and their sons and relatives—stood on the east side of the altar, dressed in fine linen and playing cymbals, harps and lyres. They were accompanied by 120 priests sounding trumpets. (2 Chronicles 5:12)

Can you imagine 120 priests blowing trumpets? What a tremendous worship service they must have had! You would not have wanted to miss "church" in those days. These were the men who performed the ministry of music within the nation of Israel.

And today in our churches we follow in their footsteps. We have choirs, orchestras, soloists, and worship bands with electric guitars, electric bass, and percussion. Why? Because we want to be entertained on Sunday mornings? No! Because music is a powerful teaching ministry. Music lifts the soul toward heaven. Music prepares the spirit for worship. And we rightfully honor those who minister through music in the church.

There is a third group mentioned in Nehemiah 11:19—the gate-keepers. In fact, there are 172 gatekeepers. They correspond to the ministry of the ushers in the church today who watch the doors. A gatekeeper, in the traditional sense, is a watcher. He looks out for people and serves them as they enter the temple or church. He helps them find their seats and answers their questions and makes sure they understand what they need to know. They open the windows when it gets too hot and close them when it is cold. The gatekeepers have an important ministry—a ministry that God himself ordained in Israel.

There were other Israelites who performed other ministries, such as the temple servants and the musicians and singers. A man named Pethahiah, a descendent of Zerah son of Judah, was the agent of the king of Persia in all matters relating to the people. In other words, he was the king's troubleshooter, who made sure there were no problems among the people—problems that might lead to unrest or rebellion.

In Nehemiah 11:25–36, Nehemiah lists a number of villages, settlements, and farm towns in the region surrounding Jerusalem. The cities mentioned ranged from the Mediterranean coast to the Jordan Valley, from the tribe of Benjamin's ancestral lands north and west of Jerusalem to the tribe of Judah's ancestral lands to the south and west. These were all towns from which the capital city of Jerusalem could expect help in times of trouble.

Here again we see a parallel to the church today. The body of Christ, the church, is scattered around the world, yet it is one unified body. As Christians, we are one with our brothers and sisters in Christ around the world. When you meet a fellow Christian from Asia or Africa or Latin America, you and that person may look very different, you may not understand each other's language, you may come from different cultures—but the moment you both realize you serve the same Lord, you will instantly have more in common with that person than with your unsaved next-door neighbor or that unsaved cousin you've known all your life.

Your church can work together with other churches on community-wide ministry efforts, even if those other churches belong to a different denomination or no denomination at all. Your church is not in competition with other churches. Any church that preaches the Word of God and proclaims the good news of Jesus Christ is a congregation of fellow believers. Your church derives support from them, and their church derives support from you.

Founded on Historical Fact

Nehemiah 12 begins with these words: "These were the priests and Levites who returned with Zerubbabel son of Shealtiel and with Joshua," followed by a series of hard-to-pronounce names. Again, our natural tendency might be to gloss over this passage, assuming there is nothing to be learned here.

In fact, the people named here were the priests and Levites who returned from Babylon in 538 BC, almost a hundred years before Nehemiah's day. This was the first return from captivity, led by the priest Zerubbabel and a Levite named Joshua (or Jeshua, not to be confused with the central figure of the book of Joshua). They led the first group of Israelites back to Jerusalem to begin rebuilding the temple.

Joshua and Jeshua are variant forms of the name Yeshua, which is the Hebrew form of the name Jesus. So this man Joshua/Jeshua, who co-led (with Zerubbabel) the Hebrews from captivity in Babylon back to Jerusalem is, in a sense, an Old Testament symbol of Jesus, who leads us out of captivity and will eventually take us to our true home in the New Jerusalem and the New Earth of Revelation 21.

The text goes on to trace the lineage of this man Joshua through a number of descendants down to a priest named Jaddua. There is an interesting controversy surrounding Jaddua, and this reference has stirred up criticism of the book of Nehemiah. Critics say this reference dates the book to a much later period of time—to the era of Alexander the Great (356 BC–323 BC), roughly a century after Nehemiah lived.

The Jewish historian Josephus tells us that when Alexander the Great led his Greek armies through the Middle East toward Egypt, he arrived at the gates of Jerusalem. His plan was to conquer Jerusalem and sack the city. But he was met by a company of priests led by a high priest whose name was Jaddua. During their meeting, Jaddua opened the scroll of the prophet Daniel and showed it to Alexander, specifically Daniel 8, where we find a prediction that a male goat with a great central horn (a clear symbol of the leader of the Greek nation) would come against the Holy Land and would conquer most of the world of that day. Alexander realized that this prediction referred to him. He was so impressed with this prophecy that he spared Jerusalem and continued on his way to conquer Egypt, where he established the city of Alexandria.

Therefore the critics of the book of Nehemiah say that this mention of the priest named Jaddua discredits the book of Nehemiah because its reference to Jaddua is off by more than a century. Unfortunately for the critics, research later revealed that there were a number of priests named Jaddua in Hebrew history. It's not hard to imagine some of these priests passing their name on to their sons, just as fathers do today. So this criticism of Nehemiah is unfounded.

What is the lesson of this passage for our lives today? Certainly, one lesson is that we must not forget our heroes of the faith. We must not forget people God has used in powerful ways down through the years. In fact, I would urge you to read biographies of great Christians of the past—Augustine of Hippo, John Wycliffe, Martin Luther, William Tyndale, Blaise Pascal, Isaac Newton,

Jonathan Edwards, Charles Wesley, John Wesley, George White-field, Francis Thomas McDougall, William Booth, Fanny Crosby, Evie Brand, Reuben Archer Torrey, Dietrich Bonhoeffer, Maximilian Kolbe, Corrie ten Boom, Jim Elliot, A. W. Tozer, C. S. Lewis, Aleksandr Solzhenitsyn, John Stott, Billy Graham, Francis Schaeffer, and others.

The lives of great Christians have impacted my life in countless ways. I call Dr. H. A. Ironside my "patron saint" because he mentored me and taught me most of what I know about being a minister of the gospel. I was privileged to travel with him for a summer before I was called to be the founding pastor of the Peninsula Bible Church. Another great Christian who impacted my life was Dr. J. Vernon McGee, the noted radio Bible teacher and scholar. I was his youth director for two summers, and he taught me countless invaluable lessons in how to study and expound the Scriptures. I have also been inspired and instructed as I have read about the lives of the founder of Dallas Seminary Dr. Lewis Sperry Chafer, missionary Hudson Taylor, and evangelist D. L. Moody.

Read the biographies of great men and women of God. Their stories will motivate you and challenge you and strengthen you to live boldly for the Lord Jesus Christ. They have stood firm against the temptations and pressures of this world, and God has used them to accomplish amazing things for His glory.

There is an interesting statement in Nehemiah 12:24. It says that "the leaders of the Levites were Hashabiah, Sherebiah, Jeshua son of Kadmiel, and their associates, who stood opposite them to give praise and thanksgiving, one section responding to the other, as prescribed by David the man of God." David lived and ruled over Israel more than five centuries before the time of Nehemiah, yet his influence over the nation was still strongly felt. Equally remarkable is the fact that David fell into sin—the sin of adultery and the murder of the woman's husband, one of his generals—yet Nehemiah calls him "David the man of God."

This is a powerful statement of the redemptive grace of God. David sinned horribly, yet he repented sincerely, and God forgave him and restored him. Yes, there were terrible consequences David had to pay because of his sin, yet he was cleansed by God's generous provision of forgiveness. That is why David is known today as the man after God's own heart (See Acts 13:22). If you need to experience the grace and forgiveness of God, study the life of David.

Verses 25 and 26 of Nehemiah 12 list the names of the gatekeepers who guarded the storerooms at the gates, adding that they served "in the days of Nehemiah the governor and of Ezra the priest, the teacher of the Law" (v. 26). What is the significance of that statement? Simply this: The events in the book of Nehemiah are not just a parable someone invented to illustrate a spiritual concept. Nehemiah is a record of God's actions in human history. It is an accounting of how God kept His promise to restore the nation of Israel after it had strayed from His commandments.

Other religions are based on questionable visions supposedly experienced by a single prophet (such as Joseph Smith or Muhammad) or the philosophical musings of some self-styled "teacher" (Gautama Buddha or Laozi or L. Ron Hubbard). But the record of the Bible is based on historical facts, not legend, not myth, not vague abstractions. The historical reliability of the Bible has been confirmed again and again by secular historians, rediscovered documents (such as the Dead Sea Scrolls), and by a continual succession of newly uncovered archaeological evidence. God has firmly grounded His truth in the great events in the history of the world.

A young friend recently told me about a conversation he had with an atheist coworker. The atheist said, "The Bible is nothing but a collection of myths. It's not the Word of God—there is no

God. Men wrote the Bible. Men invented God as an explanation for their dreams and visions. There's no more reason to believe the Bible than there is to believe in fairy tales."

"If you had actually investigated the historical record of the Bible," my young friend replied, "you wouldn't say that. You're only attacking the Bible because you want an excuse for your own rebellion. The Bible doesn't contain fairy tales; it contains facts that are recorded in history. These events took place and have been confirmed by other historical accounts outside of the Bible."

My young friend was correct, and he gave an accurate answer to this antagonistic atheist. If you take a stand for your faith on your campus, if you read your Bible on your lunch hour at the office, or if you express your faith on social media, you can expect to be attacked, mocked, and condemned. That's why it's important to have a firm foundation of Bible knowledge to back up your faith.

Many people think that faith is "belief without evidence." That's not true. Faith is trust, based on the evidence that God has provided in His Word and in the world around us. The Christian faith is based on evidence. The apostle Peter encourages us, "Always be prepared to give an answer to everyone who asks you to give the reason for the hope that you have. But do this with gentleness and respect" (1 Peter 3:15). And the way to be prepared is to know your Bible, know what you believe, and know why you believe it.

The events in the Old Testament—the reign of King David, the temple built by Solomon and destroyed by the Babylonians under Nebuchadnezzar, the Babylonian captivity, the decree of Cyrus the Great permitting the Jews to return to their homeland, the rebuilding of the walls of Jerusalem, the restoration of the temple—are all undeniable historical facts. Likewise, the events in the New Testament—the birth and ministry and execution of Jesus, the resurrection of Jesus, the conversion of Paul and the spread of the church from Jerusalem and Judea and Samaria to the uttermost parts of the earth—are undeniable historical facts.

These are great assurances to carry with us onto the campus, into the marketplace, into our neighborhoods, into the places where we live our lives and conduct our business. This is the message we proclaim to the world: We serve The King of Creation, the Lord of Salvation, and the God of History and Eternity. It is His truth we proclaim.

11

†††††††††††††††

THE SOUND OF REJOICING

Nehemiah 12:27–47

From August 1961 to November 1989, Berlin was a divided city—divided by a grim, gray concrete wall. The Soviet-installed government of East Germany built the Berlin Wall out of steel-reinforced concrete slabs, along with a series of fortified guard towers, anti-vehicle trenches, and coils of razor wire. The wall was designed to keep East Germans under the jackboot of communism. It became a tangible symbol of what Winston Churchill called the "Iron Curtain" separating communist Eastern Europe from the Free World.

Some walls, like the Berlin Wall, are instruments of oppression. But the reconstructed wall of Jerusalem was so different. It was an instrument of protection and liberation. The Berlin Wall instilled fear in the people; the Jerusalem wall gladdened the hearts of the people. The Berlin Wall divided the German people; the Jerusalem wall united the Israelites. The people of Germany celebrated the collapse and dismantling of the Berlin Wall; the people of Israel celebrated the rebuilding and dedication of the Jerusalem wall.

In the letter part of Nehemiah 12, we read the story of the dedication of the Jerusalem wall. This event was a celebration of joy and liberation for the people—liberation from fear, from intimidation, from danger, from national humiliation and disgrace. The dedication of the wall was postponed for a while until the city was repopulated. Now the wall is complete, the gates have been hung. the city is well-defended and bustling with people. The time has come to celebrate and dedicate the restored wall of Jerusalem.

The account of the dedication of the wall begins with the Levites, priests, and musicians being gathered from the towns and villages around Jerusalem. They come into the city and ceremonially purify themselves, the people, the gates, and the wall. Then Nehemiah sends the leaders of the province of Judah up onto the wall, and he assigns two choirs to lead the people in praise and thanksgiving to God. One choir proceeded to the right, and the other went to the left. Musicians played trumpets and other musical instruments—in keeping with instructions of King David five centuries before (12:45–47).

Also, the leaders take up an offering. One way you can be sure that this is a religious event is that they take an offering—you can't do anything religious without passing the plate! So this passage divides into two sections: (1) the great procession, and (2) the great offering.

The First Element of Celebration: Joy

This section of Nehemiah 12 opens with a description of the elements that make up a true celebration:

At the dedication of the wall of Jerusalem, the Levites were sought out from where they lived and were brought to Jerusalem to celebrate joyfully the dedication with songs of thanksgiving and with the music of cymbals, harps and lyres. The musicians also were brought together from the region around Jerusalem—from the villages of the Netophathites, from Beth Gilgal, and from the area of Geba and Azmaveth, for the musicians had built villages for themselves around Jerusalem. When the priests and Levites had purified themselves ceremonially, they purified the people, the gates and the wall.

I had the leaders of Judah go up on top of the wall. I also assigned two large choirs to give thanks. (Nehemiah 12:27–31)

The priests, Levites, musicians, and singers gathered to celebrate this great achievement, the rebuilding of the wall. They had come not merely to celebrate but also to dedicate. It is fine and fitting to celebrate whenever God enables us to achieve a great work. But it is even more important to dedicate that achievement to God.

Dedication is the act of consecrating something—the act of setting something apart for a special purpose. The Jerusalem wall was being consecrated for God's use and God's glory. It was more than just a defensive fortification for a city. It was a visible demonstration of God's power and His special concern for the holy city, Jerusalem.

All Scripture is inspired by God, of course, and in this account, the Spirit of God has been careful to include three elements that make up true celebration. All three elements are included in these verses. The first element is joy. Nehemiah tells us that the Levites "were brought to Jerusalem to celebrate joyfully" (v. 27). True celebration is an expression of joy, and every Christian should live out authentic Christian joy on a daily basis.

Why, then, do so many Christians seem so joyless and grim? I'm reminded of the little girl who met a mule for the first time and said, "I don't know what you are but you must be a Christian because you look just like Grandpa!" It's true—there are sometimes long-faced Christians in the church. We must strive to reflect the joy that is ours in Christ.

The atheist philosopher Friedrich Nietzsche of the nineteenth century often said that the best argument against Christianity was the joylessness of Christians.[1] In *Human, All-Too-Human*, Nietzsche offered this advice to Christians: "If your faith makes you happy, show yourselves to be happy."[2]

I'm not suggesting that Christians should go around giddy with joy all the time. There are times of sorrow and sadness in the life of every believer. Yet for the most part we should have the joy of salvation shining from our faces. We ought to exude joy for the simple reason that we have something to be joyful about.

Joy is related to happiness, but joy is not the same thing as happiness. We should not confuse the two. The people of Jerusalem were happy, they were celebrating, and they were excited. But they also felt something much deeper than mere happiness. They were experiencing joy.

Happiness is an emotional experience—a state of being exceedingly cheerful and filled with pleasure and delight because of one's circumstances at that moment. Scientists who study the physiology of happiness will tell you that a euphoric state of well-being is often the result of the release of substances called endorphins, which are generated naturally by your body. A state of happiness is momentary and fleeting. Authentic joy goes much deeper than that.

We can have joy—genuine joy—even when we are not happy, when we are not experiencing an "endorphin rush." Our emotions can go up and down depending on a change in our circumstances, and even a fluctuation in our body chemistry. But the joy of the Lord is constant and unchanging. When our hearts are right with God, we experience true joy, regardless of our circumstances.

That joy comes from knowing we are accepted and loved by God himself.

Happiness depends on happenings. Joy depends on justification. Happiness comes from without. Joy comes from within. Circumstances can produce a moment of happiness, and circumstances can steal our happiness away—but circumstances cannot rob us of our joy. Happiness fades quickly, but joy lasts forever.

The people who celebrated the completion of the walls of Jerusalem were happy that they had achieved their objective. But they weren't merely happy—they were truly joyful because they knew that God himself had enabled them to finish the work. They were joyful because they were co-laborers with God. His hand was with the project from start to finish. Yes, they were happy—but on a deeper and more important level, they were joyful.

Joy was the first element of their celebration.

The Second Element of Celebration: Purification

A clue to the second element of authentic celebration is tucked away in verse 30, which tells us that the priests and Levites "purified themselves ceremonially" before purifying the people, the gates, and the wall. We must purify ourselves before we celebrate. We cannot celebrate the works of God while there is sin and hypocrisy in our hearts. Celebration without purification is a festival of empty words. As the Psalmist reminds us:

> Who may ascend the mountain of the LORD?
>   Who may stand in his holy place?
> The one who has clean hands and a pure heart,
>   who does not trust in an idol
>   or swear by a false god.
> They will receive blessing from the LORD

and vindication from God their Savior.
Such is the generation of those who seek him,
    who seek your face, God of Jacob. (Psalm 24:3–6)

Many people in our culture today seem to fear this word *purity*. They think it describes a self-righteous and judgmental kind of person—or they think it describes someone who is naïve and excessively virtuous, a "goody two-shoes."[3] One of Satan's most successful strategies is his ability to convince people that purity is a bad thing.

Moral and spiritual purification stems from the same motivation as every other form of purity. We don't want to eat off of dirty dishes, so we purify them by washing them. We don't want to eat food with impurities, drink dirty water, breathe polluted air, or put on dirty clothes. And God does not do His work with dirty vessels. That's why purification is such an important issue throughout Scripture.

As Christians, we need a periodic cleansing of our lives and hearts. That is what the priests and Levites demonstrate to us in Nehemiah 12. First they purify themselves, because impure vessels cannot produce pure results. You would not cook a meal in a filthy pot, because the filth in the pot would contaminate your meal. In the same way, if contaminated priests and contaminated Levites try to purify the people, the gates, and the walls, they would only succeed in spreading their own moral and spiritual contamination. That's why leaders have a special obligation to purify themselves before they seek to lead, teach, and preach to the people.

Once the priests and Levites had purified themselves, they ceremonially purified the gates, the walls, and the people, because they were about to participate in a celebration of God's work. How do we purify ourselves?

In the Old Testament, outward ceremonies and rituals symbolized an inward reality of the heart. In the church today, we have largely done away with the rituals, and we have focused on the New

Testament process of purification. We confess our faults to God, to ourselves, and to trusted believers who hold us accountable. We admit our sins and failings, without making excuses, without trying to shift the blame, and without minimizing them or glossing over them. We confess that we have sinned against God. We seek forgiveness from those we have sinned against, and we seek to live every day in a right relationship with God and others.

By living lives of continuous self-examination and confession, we experience the joy of living pure and holy lives. The apostle John put it this way: "If we confess our sins, he is faithful and just and will forgive us our sins and purify us from all unrighteousness" (1 John 1:9). The more frequently and regularly we examine our lives and confess our sins, the more fully we become an instrument of God's plan. If we continually breathe out confession and breathe in forgiveness, God will send opportunities for us to minister to the people around us. He will use us in a mighty way.

The Third Element of Celebration: Thankfulness

Next we find a third element of authentic celebration embedded in this passage. Nehemiah tells us that he sent the leaders of Judah to stand on top of the wall, and he assigned two great choirs to lead the nation in thanks to God.

Thankfulness is always an ingredient of sincere celebration. And a genuine spirit of thankfulness is always expressed to God. Thankfulness is not some generalized mood of gladness. It is gratitude to God for a gift He has given us. In the United States today, families often gather on the fourth Thursday of November to eat turkey and pumpkin pie, supposedly in a spirit of "thankfulness." Yet secular people—those who have no relationship with God—really have no one to be thankful to. It's enjoyable to be with family and eat good food, but the occasion has no deeper meaning for them than that.

But the people of Jerusalem in Nehemiah's time had much to be thankful for, and they had Someone to be thankful to. They were grateful for God's influence on the part of the king of Persia, which made this project possible. They were grateful for God's protection of the workers during the rebuilding project, when they were constantly under threat. They were thankful to God for their spirit of unity and cooperation, and for the physical strength to complete the project. They were thankful to God for His generous supply of food, shelter, and protection.

So we look at the example of these Israelites and we have to ask ourselves: Are we truly thankful to God for all He has done for us? Do we give thanks every day to God for the blessings we enjoy at this very moment?

The English cleric and writer Charles Caleb Colton once said, "True contentment depends not upon what we have; a tub was large enough for Diogenes, but a world was too little for Alexander the Great." One of the signs of true Christian growth and maturity is a spirit of contentment and thankfulness to God for the blessings and liberties He has already given us.

So these are the three elements that make up true celebration of the work of God: joyfulness, purity, and thanksgiving.

Walking and Claiming

Next, Nehemiah tells us that he divided his choirs and had them march around the perimeter of the city on the top of the wall:

> I had the leaders of Judah go up on top of the wall. I also assigned two large choirs to give thanks. One was to proceed on top of the wall to the right, toward the Dung Gate. Hoshaiah and half the leaders of Judah followed them, along with Azariah, Ezra, Meshullam, Judah, Benjamin, Shemaiah, Jeremiah, as well as some priests with trumpets,

and also Zechariah son of Jonathan, the son of Shemaiah, the son of Mattaniah, the son of Micaiah, the son of Zakkur, the son of Asaph, and his associates—Shemaiah, Azarel, Milalai, Gilalai, Maai, Nethanel, Judah and Hanani—with musical instruments prescribed by David the man of God. Ezra the teacher of the Law led the procession. At the Fountain Gate they continued directly up the steps of the City of David on the ascent to the wall and passed above the site of David's palace to the Water Gate on the east. (Nehemiah 12:31–37)

One choir began on the western side of the wall, went down around the southern end of the city, and up along the eastern side where they approached the temple. The other choir took the opposite route:

The second choir proceeded in the opposite direction. I followed them on top of the wall, together with half the people—past the Tower of the Ovens to the Broad Wall, over the Gate of Ephraim, the Jeshanah Gate, the Fish Gate, the Tower of Hananel and the Tower of the Hundred, as far as the Sheep Gate. At the Gate of the Guard they stopped. (Nehemiah 12:38–39)

Setting off in opposite directions, these two choirs marched around the city until they rejoined on the eastern side of the city, before the temple. They marched with banners flying, instruments sounding, and voices singing.

This ceremony reminds me of the story of Joshua and the taking of Jericho. God told Joshua to have the people march around the city of Jericho once a day. Then, on the seventh day, they were to march around the city seven times and blow the trumpets. Joshua and the Israelites did as God commanded, and at the sound of the trumpets, the walls collapsed. The Israelites entered and took the city.

I can't say with certainty that the Jericho account inspired this ceremony, but I do see a similar principle involved: When God calls us to claim something for Him, He often calls us to walk completely around it and mark off its perimeter. In this way, we ceremonially establish God's claim and give that thing to God.

I think there may have been an element of this kind of ceremony in Nehemiah's thinking when he first arrived in Jerusalem and attempted to ride around the perimeter of Jerusalem on a donkey at night. He rode around the collapsed wall of the city, inspecting the ruins and assessing the size and scope of the task before him. He found that he was unable to go all the way around the city because his pathway was blocked by rubble. So he was unable to completely compass the city during that moonlight ride.

Though Nehemiah's ride was primarily an inspection tour, I think he may well have wanted to reclaim the city and its walls for God after it had been sacked by the pagan Babylonians. Only now—only after the walls had been completely rebuilt and dedicated—could Nehemiah complete this ceremonial encirclement of Jerusalem and reclaim the city for God.

Another instance of God telling His people to walk around a place and claim it for Him was in Genesis, when God told Abraham to walk around the Land of Promise: "Go, walk through the length and breadth of the land, for I am giving it to you" (Genesis 13:17).

So we should ask ourselves: "Have I ever, by faith, walked around a situation and claimed it for God? Have I ever prayed my way all around every aspect of some need in order to claim it in God's name and asked Him to give it to me?"

I'm not suggesting that we should be presumptuous. I'm not saying that there is magical power in walking around a piece of property and claiming it because we want it. Some TV preachers suggest that you can name and claim a luxury car or a mansion in God's name, and God will give it to you (especially if you donate generously to that preacher). There is no biblical basis for such a notion. Abraham didn't tell God, "Lord, give me the land that I am going to walk around." No, God told Abraham to walk the land "for I am giving it to you." Abraham walked the land in accordance with the promise that God had already given to him. God has given us more than 3,000 promises in His Word, and we can safely and confidently lay claim to any of those promises in His name.

If you are facing a serious problem in your marriage, your family, your business, or your church, you need wisdom to deal with that problem—and God has promised, "If any of you lacks wisdom, you should ask God, who gives generously to all without finding fault, and it will be given to you" (James 1:5). You can figuratively "walk around" the circumference of the problem you face, naming every aspect of that problem and lifting it up to God, asking God for His wisdom for that problem, and He has promised to give you the wisdom you need.

God has promised to send us bountiful blessings, including blessings on our children and victory over our enemies, if we obey the Lord our God (see Deuteronomy 28:2–8). We should "walk around" our lives and look at all the aspects of our lives—our devotional life with God, our moral life that no one sees, our behavior toward family members and coworkers and the people all around us—and we should ask God to help us to live obedient lives before God, so that we can lay claim to His promise of blessing in our lives.

And God has promised to bless the people around us, making our households a "holy hill" of blessing to the world (see Ezekiel 34:26). Perhaps you would want to "walk around" the "holy hill" of your home and claim this promise for your life and your family. You could ask God to make your home a beacon of His light to your neighbors and friends and to all who come to your doorstep. Walk around your home, your apartment, your family members, and claim them for God, in accordance with the promises He has already given you.

The Lord may bring other promises to mind. Consider the example of Nehemiah and the example of Abraham. Claim the promises God has already made to you, and either figuratively or physically walk around the promise God has given you and celebrate His gracious blessings in your life.

Tools in the Master's Workshop

Next, Nehemiah tells us that the choirs joined together and entered the temple for a great service of thanksgiving:

> The two choirs that gave thanks then took their places in the house of God; so did I, together with half the officials, as well as the priests—Eliakim, Maaseiah, Miniamin, Micaiah, Elioenai, Zechariah and Hananiah with their trumpets—and also Maaseiah, Shemaiah, Eleazar, Uzzi, Jehohanan, Malkijah, Elam and Ezer. The choirs sang under the direction of Jezrahiah. And on that day they offered great sacrifices, rejoicing because God had given them great joy. The women and children also rejoiced. The sound of rejoicing in Jerusalem could be heard far away. (Nehemiah 12:40–43)

All the families of the province of Judah—men, women, and children—rejoiced as one over what God had accomplished through them in rebuilding and repopulating the city of Jerusalem. They offered sacrifices—thank offerings as prescribed by the Law as an expression of gratitude to God. The New Testament tells us that there is a correspondence between the sacrifices of Nehemiah's day and the sacrifice we are to make as Christians today: "Through Jesus, therefore, let us continually offer to God a sacrifice of praise—the fruit of lips that openly profess his name. And do not forget to do good and to share with others, for with such sacrifices God is pleased" (Hebrews 13:15–16).

Praising God, doing good, and sharing with others—these are the sacrifices of thanksgiving that God wants from us today. If we praise God for what He has done, and if we share generously with others—always doing good to them—then God will be honored. Plus, He will be pleased with our sacrifice of thanksgiving to Him.

A man in our church once told me from his own experience about how God's people in our church offered a generous sacrifice of sharing with his family. This man's wife came from another culture, and when they came into our church, she didn't know anyone in the congregation. She was expecting a baby, and after the baby was born, a group of women from our congregation volunteered to bring meals for the family. Every night for a month, this woman could focus solely on caring for her newborn baby because she never had to think about preparing dinner. This man and his wife were amazed and blessed by the sacrifice of sharing our congregation offered to them—and to God.

This is the kind of sacrifice that pleases God. This is the kind of love He calls us to.

In the closing verses of Nehemiah 12, we read about the great offering that was taken up in the worship service at the temple:

> At that time men were appointed to be in charge of the storerooms for the contributions, firstfruits and tithes. From the fields around the towns they were to bring into the storerooms the portions required by the Law for the priests and the Levites, for Judah was pleased with the ministering priests and Levites. They performed the service of their God and the service of purification, as did also the musicians and gatekeepers, according to the commands of David and his son Solomon. For long ago, in the days of David and Asaph, there had been directors for the musicians and for the songs of praise and thanksgiving to God. So in the days of Zerubbabel and of Nehemiah, all Israel contributed the daily portions for the musicians and the

gatekeepers. They also set aside the portion for the other Levites, and the Levites set aside the portion for the descendants of Aaron. (Nehemiah 12:44–47)

Nehemiah tells us three significant facts about these offerings. These three insights are directly applicable and relevant to our lives today.

The first insight: Nehemiah tells us that these offerings were given out of the spirit of pleasure. The people of the province of Judah were "pleased with the ministering priests and Levites." Both the Old Testament and the New Testament confirm that our offerings mean nothing if they are not given cheerfully. The apostle Paul wrote, "Each of you should give what you have decided in your heart to give, not reluctantly or under compulsion, for God loves a cheerful giver" (2 Corinthians 9:7). The original Greek word that is translated cheerful is the root word from which we get our English word hilarious—so in a sense, God truly wants people to give hilariously. He wants givers who laugh and shout with joy as they give back a portion of what God has given to them.

If you do not give with a thrill of joyfulness as your motive, then God is not interested in your gift. He doesn't care how big or how small it is, because he already owns the whole world. He cares about the attitude of your heart as you give. Jesus tells us that a widow who donated two tiny copper coins, the smallest and least valuable coins in circulation in that day, gave more than all the rich people who cast sacks-full of gold into the treasury. Why? Because she gave with pleasure out of a pure love for God. The rich gave so their wealth and phony "generosity" might be noticed by all their neighbors and friends. God always looks for the one who takes pleasure in giving, the one who gives hilariously out of a thankful heart.

My mentor, Dr. H. A. Ironside, told the story of an old Scotsman who placed a coin in the collection bag at a church service. In Scotland, the ushers used a long pole with a bag on the end to take up the offering among the pews. The old Scotsman meant to put in only a shilling, but he dropped in a gold sovereign by mistake—and he only realized his mistake as he watched the gold sovereign fall into the bag. Instantly, he grabbed hold of the bag and tried to retrieve his sovereign.

The usher yanked the bag back and said, "Nah, once in, always in!"

The old man said, "Ah well, I'll get credit for it in glory."

The usher replied, "Nah, ye'll get credit for the shilling!"

God gives us credit for the heart's intent, not our donation's "purchasing power" or "spot exchange rate." To paraphrase the Lord's words in 1 Samuel 16:7: "Man looks at the financial balance sheet, but the Lord looks at the heart.

The second insight: Nehemiah tells us that these offerings were given "according to the commands of David and his son Solomon." David and Solomon lived five centuries before Nehemiah, so these instructions and traditions had been in force twice as long as the United States of America has been a country. To translate this timescale to our own time, it would be as if we were observing rules and traditions that went back to the days of Christopher Columbus and William Shakespeare.

The commands of David and Solomon included instructions in how the priests, the Levites, the musicians, and the gatekeepers were to be purified for service and were to perform their function. All who took part in the worship service were to be purified not only ceremonially but also spiritually. They were to examine themselves to make sure they were conducting the service not to please themselves or to glorify themselves but to please and glorify God. They were to cleanse themselves from selfish ambition and self-centered pride.

People in the public eye are easily tempted to act from wrong motives. This is still a danger for us in the church today. We who have a serving role in the church—and all leaders need to see leadership as serving—should always be aware of the absolute necessity of serving with purified motives.

Serving God and serving the people through the ministry of worship is a great privilege—and a great tradition. I have been grateful over the years to have been in ministry with so many excellent musicians who have ministered in our church out of a selfless and self-effacing love for God and His people. I have seen their genuine humility—their desire to step out of the limelight and allow God alone to be glorified. This is a great tradition of worship ministry that goes back to the days of David and Solomon.

It is a sin and a grievous error to misuse a worship service in order to glorify oneself. Although I do not judge the heart of any individual—only God knows the human heart—I have seen many performances of so-called "ministry" where it was not clear to me who was being glorified. We who have a visible role in leading worship in the church have a solemn responsibility to search our hearts on a daily, even hourly, basis. We have an obligation to purify ourselves for this all-important work of the ministry.

The third insight: Nehemiah tells us that the people set aside a portion for the other Levites and priests (descendants of Aaron). The people were careful to provide for those who could not be there, or who were busy performing their ministry and did not have an opportunity to share in the offerings. This is a beautiful picture of the oneness of the nation of Israel.

God continually taught the people of Israel that they belonged to each other. They were not rugged individualists, each doing his or her own thing. They were coworkers with one another and with God. They belonged to one another, and they had an obligation to care for one another.

I know of no more important truth in the body of Christ than the recognition that God uses all of us in community with one another.

He deliberately puts us together with people who are different from ourselves—people with different gifts, different backgrounds, different viewpoints, different ethnicity and skin color. He wants us to recognize that we are all one in the body of Christ, and He calls us not merely to tolerate one another, but to embrace one another and love one another.

A number of years ago, a writer named R. T. Moore wrote a parable called "The Carpenter's Tools." Here's my paraphrase of that tale:

The Carpenter's tools gathered for a conference. Brother Hammer chaired the meeting—but there was an uprising among the tools. They objected to Brother Hammer because he was too noisy, and they said he must leave the meeting.

Brother Hammer angrily responded, "All right, if that's the way you want it, I'll go! But if you're kicking me out, you should kick Brother Screwdriver out as well. He can't drive a nail as nicely as I can—you have to turn him around and around to get him anywhere!"

Brother Screwdriver said, "If you kick me out, Brother Sandpaper must go as well. He's so superficial, there's no depth to his work! Besides, he's always rubbing others the wrong way!"

Brother Sandpaper said, "Well, if I have to go, Brother Ruler should certainly go! Who does he think he is, always measuring people as if he was the only one who's right?"

Brother Ruler was about to protest when the door of the workshop opened, and the Carpenter of Nazareth walked in to work on his latest project, a pulpit for preaching the Good News to the poor. Over the next few hours, the Carpenter used Brother Hammer, Brother Screwdriver, Brother Sandpaper, Brother Ruler, and many other tools in the workshop.

When the Carpenter had finished, there stood a beautiful pulpit, fit for the ministry of God's Word. So Brother Saw arose and, in a humble voice, said, "Brothers and sisters, it seems that we are all laborers together, tools in the hands of the Master—and not one of us is more important than the other, nor should any of us be made to feel unwelcome in the Master's workshop."

It is the Carpenter who uses us for His purpose. And we have no business finding fault with one of God's tools. Instead, we should care for one another and seek the best for one another. We should support one another as we celebrate and worship together.

So let us celebrate with joy, with purity, with thanksgiving to God, and with genuine love for one another in the body of Christ.

12

†††††††††††††††

REPORT FOR DUTY

Nehemiah 13:1–14

"And they lived happily ever after."

We all love stories with happy endings. Unfortunately, that is not how the book of Nehemiah ends. If only the book had ended with the great celebration of Nehemiah 12. If only the final chapter of the story had been all about the dedication of the walls, the shouts of joy, the songs of praise and thanksgiving, and a glorious worship service in the temple.

Instead, the book of Nehemiah continues with a thirteenth and final chapter, which records the backward slide of the people, away from their promise to serve and obey God. The trouble actually begins on the very day of the dedication of the wall. Let's read Nehemiah's account of that day:

> On that day the Book of Moses was read aloud in the hearing of the
> people and there it was found written that no Ammonite or Moabite

217

should ever be admitted into the assembly of God, because they had not met the Israelites with food and water but had hired Balaam to call a curse down on them. (Our God, however, turned the curse into a blessing.) When the people heard this law, they excluded from Israel all who were of foreign descent. (Nehemiah 13:1–3)

You'll recall that when we looked at Nehemiah 10, we saw that the people of Israel made a commitment to God and to one another that they would not intermarry with unbelievers: "We promise not to give our daughters in marriage to the peoples around us or take their daughters for our sons" (Nehemiah 10:30).

God wanted to keep His people pure and undefiled by the degenerate religious and sexual practices of the surrounding cultures—practices that included torture, human sacrifice, infant sacrifice, and the worship of the sexual organs. To protect His people, God had forbidden intermarriage with these pagan cultures.

Whenever God's people violated His command and intermingled with pagans, those cultures corrupted God's people. The Israelites repeatedly fell into the same degraded practices the pagans practiced. Here, in Nehemiah 13, we see the Israelite people apparently obeying God and excluding the Ammonites and Moabites from their assembly. These two pagan cultures inhabited the region on the eastern side of the Dead Sea, where the nation of Jordan is today.

If these events were taking place today, you might see Ammonites and Moabites holding a demonstration march, carrying placards saying, "Ammonites and Moabites demand equal rights!" And many people would support the protesters and claim that anyone denying their "equal rights" is a fascist and a racist.

But race is not the issue here. The issue is the purity of the faith. Many people would have you believe that all cultures are morally equal, and no culture should ever be criticized, condemned, or excluded. But it's foolish to say that all cultures are equal. A culture that sacrifices its children to the flames of a demon-god is not the moral equivalent of a culture that loves, protects, and defends its children. A culture that murders innocent people in the name of religion is not the moral equivalent of a culture that sends food, construction help, money, and medical missionaries to distant lands, expecting nothing in return. Everything God did in the Old Testament and the New Testament was wise, just, loving, and compassionate. All of His commands are intended to protect and heal us, not to hurt us.

The Struggle with the Flesh

The people listened to the book of Numbers, chapters 22 through 24, which contains the story of the wicked prophet Balaam. As they listened, they heard why the Ammonites and Moabites were to be excluded from the assembly of God. When the Israelites left Egypt and came to the edge of the Promised Land, into the country of the Ammonites and Moabites, the pagan inhabitants did not offer them the normal desert hospitality of food and drink. Instead, they hired the prophet Balaam to curse the nation of Israel.

Balaam is remembered for the incident when he was riding to a hilltop, planning to curse Israel. An angel that only the donkey could see appeared. The donkey refused to go on, and Balaam beat the donkey, which miraculously spoke to Balaam. Then God permitted Balaam to see the angel, who told Balaam that he would have chosen to kill the sinful prophet. But for the donkey's sake, he spared him.

Balaam later betrayed the Israelite people, counseling King Balak to seduce Israel by offering prostitutes and food sacrificed to idols, which led the people of Israel into sexual immorality and idolatry with the Moabite women. As a result, Israel was judged for its sin.

We do not understand God's ways, and we take a great risk when we insist on going our own way and ignoring God's will and purpose for our lives. He has good reasons for every commandment in His

Word, and we will save ourselves a great deal of pain and regret if we follow His will instead of insisting on going our own way.

When did the incident of Balaam and the donkey take place? When was Israel mistreated by the Ammonites and the Moabites? These events occurred nine hundred years before Nehemiah's time. You might wonder: Did God hold a grudge against the Ammonites and the Moabites for nine hundred years? Many atheists and secular critics of the Bible seize on God's judgment against these foreign tribes in order to depict God as cruel and vindictive. They accuse God of placing people under a curse and unjustly keeping them under that curse for centuries. What they perceive as God's "unfairness" is offensive to their human sense of "justice."

Have you ever felt that God was unfair? Have you ever disagreed with the judgments of God that are recorded in the Bible? We often forget that God is able to read the hearts of men and women. He knows the hidden attitudes and motives of these people. We cannot judge accurately as God judges—and that is why we're so quick to misjudge God and accuse Him of injustice.

But if we take a closer look at this story, we will see that God had very good reasons for warning the Israelites to keep the Ammonites and Moabites out of their assembly. In Ezra 9, there is an account of a similar situation that arose thirty years before Nehemiah's day. Ezra had led a group of Israelites out of Babylon and back to Jerusalem. He discovered that the people were intermarrying with pagan tribes. Here is Ezra's account:

> After these things had been done, the leaders came to me and said, "The people of Israel, including the priests and the Levites, have not kept themselves separate from the neighboring peoples with their detestable practices, like those of the Canaanites, Hittites, Perizzites, Jebusites, Ammonites, Moabites, Egyptians and Amorites. They have taken some of their daughters as wives for themselves and their sons, and have

mingled the holy race with the peoples around them. And the leaders and officials have led the way in this unfaithfulness." (Ezra 9:1–2)

The intermarrying of Israelites with the surrounding pagan tribes was a cause of great distress to Ezra. If you read the whole account, you will see that he was appalled to the point of speechlessness because of this violation of God's commandments. In the midst of his prayer, he adds these words,

"But now, our God, what can we say after this? For we have forsaken the commands you gave through your servants the prophets when you said: 'The land you are entering to possess is a land polluted by the corruption of its peoples. By their detestable practices they have filled it with their impurity from one end to the other. Therefore, do not give your daughters in marriage to their sons or take their daughters for your sons. Do not seek a treaty of friendship with them at any time, that you may be strong and eat the good things of the land and leave it to your children as an everlasting inheritance.'" (vv. 10–12)

Once we understand the morally and spiritually polluted nature of the surrounding cultures, it becomes clear that God was trying to quarantine His people against a deadly spiritual infection. These same principles apply to our lives today. We must never forget that the stories of the Old Testament are God's visual aid to teach His people vital spiritual and moral lessons. The apostle Paul tells us, "These things happened to them as examples and were written down as warnings for us, on whom the culmination of the ages has come" (1 Corinthians 10:11).

What do these stories reveal about our lives today? If you trace the Ammonites and the Moabites back to their beginnings, you will discover that they are relatives of the Israelites. Ammon and Moab, the founders of these countries, were the sons of Lot, the nephew of Abraham. During the destruction of the cities of Sodom and

Gomorrah, as fire and brimstone rained down upon these wicked cities, angels led Lot and his family up onto the mountainside. Lot's wife looked back and was turned into a pillar of salt, but Lot and his two daughters hid in a cave in the mountain while the cities burned before them.

In the aftermath of this destruction, there is a sordid incident in which Lot's daughters, evidently believing that they were the last two women on earth, deceived their father into having incestuous relations with them. They both conceived and bore sons, one named Ammon and the other named Moab. These two men founded tribes and nations by those names. So Ammon and Moab are relatives— and sworn enemies—of the Israelites.

We can choose our friends, but we can't choose our relatives. And the Israelites' relatives, the Ammonites and Moabites, were nothing but trouble. Evidently, Israelite men found the women of those tribes to be attractive—yet the foreign women brought their religious practices into the marriage with them. When Israelite men were not being seduced by the women of those tribes, they were often at war with the men of those tribes. The Ammonites and Moabites constantly harassed, corrupted, polluted, and undermined Israel. Yet God did not permit Israel to destroy these tribes because the Ammonites and Moabites were related to the Israelites.

What does this mean for us today? The New Testament tells us that we have an enemy very much like the Ammonites and Moabites. It's an enemy we are related to—and it's called "the flesh." This is our old sin nature that we inherited as children of Adam. The flesh is that inner principle of self-centeredness and self-will that afflicts us all. Whenever I want to know what my greatest problem in life is, I simply have to look in the mirror. This is true of all of us.

There is something within us that seeks to be king, to be the absolute sovereign of our lives, to rebel against our Lord and Creator. That something is the flesh. It seeks to be served, to be obeyed, to be totally in charge. The flesh wants to put self on the throne of our lives, where God alone belongs.

When we are in close fellowship with God, we are horrified by the works of the flesh. We see how the flesh leads us away from God and how it causes us to harm ourselves and others. We wish we could reach inside, ripped the sinful flesh out of us, and rid ourselves of it forever. But we cannot. The flesh is related to us, and we will struggle with it throughout our lives. God calls us to live in victory over the flesh by walking in the Spirit, but our struggle with the flesh will never be over as long as we are in these bodies.

The Temple Defiled

Nehemiah goes on to describe what takes place when he leaves Jerusalem for a time and returns to the service of the king of Persia:

> Before this, Eliashib the priest had been put in charge of the storerooms of the house of our God. He was closely associated with Tobiah, and he had provided him with a large room formerly used to store the grain offerings and incense and temple articles, and also the tithes of grain, new wine and olive oil prescribed for the Levites, musicians and gatekeepers, as well as the contributions for the priests.
>
> But while all this was going on, I was not in Jerusalem, for in the thirty-second year of Artaxerxes king of Babylon I had returned to the king. Some time later I asked his permission and came back to Jerusalem. Here I learned about the evil thing Eliashib had done in providing Tobiah a room in the courts of the house of God. I was greatly displeased and threw all Tobiah's household goods out of the

room. I gave orders to purify the rooms, and then I put back into them the equipment of the house of God, with the grain offerings and the incense. (Nehemiah 13:4–9)

So Tobiah turns up once again. This is the same Tobiah, the wicked Ammonite official, who plotted against Nehemiah and attempted to halt the rebuilding of the Jerusalem walls. Nehemiah leaves Jerusalem for an extended time and returns to his old job in Susa as an aide to the king of Persia. When he returns, he discovers that Eliashib the priest is in league with his old nemesis, Tobiah.

These kinds of political intrigues and strange alliances are much like what goes on in Washington, D.C., where politicians revile each other in front of the news cameras, but are friends and cronies in backrooms and cocktail parties. The last person in the world Eliashib the priest should be allied with was Tobiah the Ammonite—yet Eliashib had set Tobiah up with an apartment in the temple storerooms. Why would Eliashib defile God's house that way?

Nehemiah records, "One of the sons of Joiada son of Eliashib the high priest was son-in-law to Sanballat the Horonite" (Nehemiah 13:28). So Eliashib's grandson had married into the family of Sanballat the Horonite, the close political ally of Tobiah the Ammonite. This cozy alliance between Sanballat and Eliashib the priest allowed Tobiah to take up residence in a storeroom that was set apart for the grain, oil, and incense used by the Levites in their purification ceremonies. Sanballat and Tobiah were the sworn enemies of Nehemiah and the sworn enemies of God.

After the nation had pledged itself to maintain its moral and spiritual purity, and to stop intermarrying with idolatrous pagans, the grandson of the high priest had entered into one of these forbidden marriages. The result: An enemy of God, a pagan idol worshiper, was allowed to live in God's temple, defiling the temple in violation of the law of Moses—and the high priest himself was the traitor who permitted it. In addition, Eliashib had defrauded the Levites, depriving them of the right to store the grain and other items in their rightful storerooms.

When Nehemiah returned and learned of this outrage, he immediately took action. Nehemiah made no attempt to hide his anger and disgust at the priest's desecration of God's house. He wrote, "I was greatly displeased and threw all Tobiah's household goods out of the room." Then he purified the room and returned it to its proper function as a sacred storehouse for oil, grain, and incense.

Some people look at this story and accuse Nehemiah of overreacting. Many people today don't understand why anyone should be angry over Eliashib's disrespect for the temple. So he did a favor for a friend and let him live in the temple storeroom. Is that so wrong? Wasn't it also wrong for Nehemiah to lose his temper the way he did?

The reason people often feel this way today is that we have largely lost our ability to feel outrage over actions that are morally and spiritually outrageous. We have lost the ability to view sin the way God views it. In fact, in our culture today, people generally stand up for indecency and depravity while condemning those who take a moral stand.

If a filmmaker makes a motion picture that slanders and blasphemes the Lord Jesus, he will be hailed as a visionary and a genius; but should a person make a motion picture that treats the gospel story with reverence and respect, that person will be hated and ridiculed in the media. Those who reap obscene profits from abortion mills are hailed as defenders of "choice" in the media today—but if someone takes a compassionate moral stand against the killing of unborn babies, he or she will be labeled "anti-choice" and an enemy of "women's health."

Injustice makes God angry. It should make us angry as well. Nehemiah was right to become angry over this insult to God's house. Nehemiah did not lose his temper. He found his righteous indignation—and he exercised it appropriately. He lived out the words of the psalmist, who said, "For zeal for your house consumes me, and the insults of those who insult you fall on me" (Psalm 69:9).

In fact, the scene where Nehemiah tosses out Tobiah and his belongings is much like the scene in the New Testament where Jesus went to Jerusalem and cleared the merchants and moneychangers from the temple. Jesus saw wicked men making an extravagant income by commercializing the worship of God, selling sacrifices, and exchanging Roman money for temple currency. So Jesus made a whip and acted in much the same way Nehemiah did—passionately upsetting tables, driving out the corrupt men, and cleansing the temple of its defilers.

Many pacifists like to picture Jesus as gentle, humble, and mild, and He is all of that—but we must embrace the full spectrum of the Lord's personality. He is compassionate toward the hurting and oppressed—and He is passionate against those who cause hurt and oppression. If evil and injustice do not stir us, make us passionate, and fill us with indignation, then we are too lax and indulgent toward sin.

This doesn't mean we can justify our own anger and violent deeds by saying, "I was just following the Lord's example." Few of us have the wisdom and perspective to find the perfect balance of righteousness and indignation that characterized the anger of Jesus in the temple. Our anger all too easily flies out of control—so we must be very controlled in the way we express our anger. But there is a time to take a strong stand against evil—especially when the people around us accept and embrace evil and injustice as "normal."

This story in Nehemiah 13 reveals clearly how evil works. Sin is subtle, and it invades us quietly and covertly. Before we are even aware of the danger, we have already compromised ourselves and given evil a place in our hearts. We lower our defenses—and soon we have lowered our standards. We seldom fall suddenly into sin. Our descent into sin is almost always gradual—the culmination of a lot of seemingly insignificant choices. As C. S. Lewis observed in *The Screwtape Letters*, "The safest road to hell is the gradual one— the gentle slope, soft underfoot, without sudden turnings, without milestones, without signposts."[1]

That's why it's so important for us to regularly take stock of our lives. We need to fearlessly examine ourselves and ask ourselves, "Am I truly walking with God—or am I walking on that gradual downward slope that leads to my own destruction?" In fact, we should all have a few trusted Christian friends in our lives—people we can open our lives to and confess our faults to. We need people we can trust to speak the truth in love and yank us back from the flames of our own sin and self-destruction.

Sin easily enters our lives through the weakness and willfulness of the flesh. Like Tobiah, sin moves in and takes up residence in the temple of our spirit, polluting and destroying us in the process. Remember the warning of Jesus in the Sermon on the Mount:

> "If your right eye causes you to stumble, gouge it out and throw it away. It is better for you to lose one part of your body than for your whole body to be thrown into hell. And if your right hand causes you to stumble, cut it off and throw it away. It is better for you to lose one part of your body than for your whole body to go into hell." (Matthew 5:29–30)

If sin has begun to take up residence in your life—the sin of lust, pride, bitterness, envy, gossip, hate, lying, stealing—then deal with it. Take immediate action, just as Nehemiah took action against Tobiah. Don't allow evil to take up residence in your temple. Don't tolerate sin. That's the lesson of Nehemiah's example.

As Nehemiah continued to investigate what had taken place while he was away from Jerusalem, he discovered other injustices that had caused God's house to be neglected. Nehemiah writes:

> I also learned that the portions assigned to the Levites had not been given to them, and that all the Levites and musicians responsible for the service had gone back to their own fields. So I rebuked the officials and asked them, "Why is the house of God neglected?" Then I called them together and stationed them at their posts.
>
> All Judah brought the tithes of grain, new wine and olive oil into the storerooms. (Nehemiah 13:10–12)

This neglect of the temple is a direct result of the practice of intermarrying with the Ammonites and Moabites. When Tobiah moved into the temple storehouse, the Levites had to throw out the grain, oil, and incense they needed to perform their ministry. When they were no longer adequately supported, they went to work in the fields in order to support themselves. As a result, the services of the temple were neglected.

Transposing the lessons of Nehemiah 13 to our own lives, we can see a similar principle at work. If we allow prayer and the Scriptures to be displaced from our lives, we will quickly begin to neglect the worship of God. Enticing lusts and sinful habits will take the place in our lives that rightfully belongs to God.

The solution is drastic action. That is what Nehemiah did. He rebuked the officials who allowed the temple to be neglected. He called them together and restored them to their place of ministry. He insisted that the people obey the Scriptures, and he called upon them to bring in the tithes and the oil and incense once more, so that the storehouses of the temple would be full again. In this way, Nehemiah restored order, health, and life to the nation.

Four Indispensable Qualities

Nehemiah goes on to describe the positive actions he took to safeguard the integrity of the ministry in the temple—and being a man of prayer, he adds a word of supplication to God:

> I put Shelemiah the priest, Zadok the scribe, and a Levite named Pedaiah in charge of the storerooms and made Hanan son of Zakkur, the son of Mattaniah, their assistant, because they were considered trustworthy. They were made responsible for distributing the supplies to their fellow Levites. Remember me for this, my God, and do not blot out what I have so faithfully done for the house of my God and its services. (Nehemiah 13:13–14)

To safeguard the purity and integrity of the temple, Nehemiah selects a priest, a scribe, a Levite, and a layman. These four individuals represent four aspects of the life of Israel, yet they share one great quality. Nehemiah tells us, "they were considered trustworthy." They were faithful men of proven character.

Today, we tend to pay lip service to trustworthy character, yet we don't highly esteem it in practice. We say we want integrity and honesty in our leaders, yet we keep electing people of questionable character because they tell us what we want to hear. It is disheartening to see how hard it is to find faithful leaders in our communities, our corporations, our government, and yes, our churches. Few people take seriously the responsibility to be faithful servants of God.

God continually seeks a few good men and women who will live faithfully for Him. The apostle Paul tells us that those who minister in the church are "servants of Christ" who have been "entrusted with the mysteries God has revealed. Now it is required that those who have been given a trust must prove faithful" (see 1 Corinthians 4:1–2).

What is faithfulness? It is the willingness to fulfill a responsibility, day after day, year after year, without needing to be asked, without demanding praise or thanks, but simply showing up again and again to do God's work until the work is done. That's what it means to be faithful, and that quality is all too rare in the world today.

David Roper, a former associate pastor in our church (Peninsula Bible Church), wrote a book called *The Strength of a Man*. In the introduction, he writes:

> Most of my friends consider themselves real men. They're outdoorsmen and sportsmen. They hunt and fish. They hang their snowmobiles upside down under the snow cornices on West Mountain. They hie themselves across the desert in 4x4s at what I consider terminal velocities. I have one friend who pulled a grizzly bear off of his wife with his bare hands. I saw another ride a log down a canyon wall. He almost broke the sound barrier on the way down; he did break two ribs at the bottom. But to hear him tell it, it was the thrill of a lifetime.
>
> Yet for all our macho, we men are mostly uneasy about our manhood. None of us seems to know for sure what it means. We have to be told: Real men don't eat quiche. They don't bunt. They don't have "meaningful dialogues." And rarely do they think about the meaning of life. Real men love John Wayne, Monday Night Football, chain saws, and Coors.[2]

David Roper rang the bell on the way many (perhaps most) men would define manhood. But this is not Nehemiah's definition of manhood. He is not looking for someone with a macho attitude, someone who can wrestle a grizzly bear or ride a log down a mountainside. Nehemiah is looking for *someone who is faithful*. God honors faithfulness. God rewards those who serve Him faithfully in this life. Jesus has promised that God will one day say, after we have served Him faithfully throughout our lives, "Well done, good and faithful servant! . . . Come and share your master's happiness!" (see Matthew 25:21).

Over the years, whenever I have sought qualified candidates for ministry and leadership, whether men or women, I have learned to look for four specific qualities:

Quality No. 1: A searching mind. I have learned to seek out people who are mentally alert, who are curious about life, and who are committed to lifelong learning. I seek out people who are always reading, always listening, and always thinking about the ideas and insights they have heard. They don't accept anything at face value but continually search out the deeper reality of everything. A great leader, a great servant, has a searching mind.

Quality No. 2: A humble heart. Egotism and pride are dangerous qualities in a leader. Prideful people are not really in ministry—they are performers seeking applause. They don't understand the privilege of serving quietly and anonymously. They don't understand the importance of performing for an Audience of One. Leadership is a burden that only the humble can carry. That's why Jesus said, "Whoever wants to become great among you must be your servant, and whoever wants to be first must be slave of all. For even the Son of Man did not come to be served, but to serve, and to give his life as a ransom for many" (Mark 10:43–45). A humble heart is a non-negotiable qualification for leadership.

Quality No. 3: An evident gift. God's people are gifted people. There is not one member of the body of Christ who has not been equipped for ministry by the Holy Spirit. When we recognize our spiritual gift and we use it for God's glory, we take delight in serving the Lord. A spiritual gift is not a burden to the believer, any more than the gift of flight is a burden to a bird. When seeking leaders and servants for the ministry in the church, I look for people who know their gift and enjoy using it in ministry.

Quality No. 4: A faithful spirit. A person who is truly faithful does not quit. Faithful people did not lose heart, but they trust God to give them the strength to keep going. That's the kind of person Nehemiah put in charge of the ministry of the temple. That's the kind of person we should always seek for positions of leadership and service.

Not only are these four qualities present in the people Nehemiah chose but these qualities are also reflected in Nehemiah's own life. He had a searching mind, a humble heart, a gift of administration and leadership, and a faithful spirit. He was committed to carrying out God's will, and he refused to let anything stop him. He refused to let opposition discourage him. He refused to let obstacles get in his way.

It amazes me that in all of Israel, no one could be found to undertake the project of rebuilding the walls and gates of Jerusalem. It took a man from the far-off kingdom of Persia to journey to Jerusalem and lead the rebuilding effort. At great personal cost, Nehemiah undertook the project and saw it through to completion. He never quit, he never slowed down, he pressed on against all odds. That is the lesson of the book of Nehemiah.

God is looking for people in every age who will be faithful to the end, who will be agents of change. He is not merely looking for highly visible leaders, such as pastors or authors or speakers. God is looking for people who will be faithful in ministry in their shops and homes, their offices and campuses, their teams and platoons. God is looking for people who will minister right where they are and who will be faithful to the end.

A Humble Prayer

When we read the prayer of Nehemiah in chapter 13, verse 14, we are reading the prayer of a faithful servant of God. Some people think Nehemiah sounds a bit self-serving in this prayer: "Remember me for this, my God, and do not blot out what I have so faithfully done for the house of my God and its services." I don't agree that this prayer is in any way self-serving. I think Nehemiah is actually demonstrating great humility in this prayer. He recognizes his own fallenness and fallibility, and he worries that, after serving God faithfully, there might be some hidden character flaw, some fatal tendency to sin that would result in Nehemiah being blotted out of God's book. And Nehemiah feared his own sin nature more than he feared his mortal enemies.

That is what Nehemiah was asking in this prayer—and that is why it is clear to me that Nehemiah had a genuinely humble heart. The prayer Nehemiah prays is much like the prayer of David at the end of Psalm 139:

> Search me, God, and know my heart;
>> test me and know my anxious thoughts.
> See if there is any offensive way in me,
>> and lead me in the way everlasting. (vv. 23–24)

This is an honest prayer, prayed by a man of God—a faithful man of God throughout most of his life, but a man who was once tested and who tragically failed that test. King David, more than most of us, knew the depths of the moral and spiritual failure he was capable of. He had gone to those depths, he had committed adultery, and he had tried to cover up that sin with murder.

Yet he repented of his sin, and God restored him to leadership and ministry as king of Israel. He and others paid a terrible price for his sin. Yet he persevered with God, and he remained faithful to the end. That is the same faithfulness and perseverance that Nehemiah demonstrates when he prays, "Do not blot out what I have so faithfully done for the house of my God and its services."

May that be our prayer as we seek to be faithful leaders and servants and ministers in this crucial moment in history. We all have a ministry to perform, a calling to fulfill, in our homes, our churches, our communities, our world. Every day, we rub shoulders with people who are lost, hurting, and spiritually bankrupt. They won't come into our churches. But God has sent us out into their world. He calls us to reach out to them, wherever we are.

God is calling your name right now. Will you answer? Will you report for duty? Will you be faithful to the end?

13

††††††††††††††††

PREVENTING BURNOUT AND PRESERVING POWER

Nehemiah 13:15—31

Jennifer missed her daddy.

No, her daddy wasn't away on a trip. In fact, he was home every night. But night after night, he brought home a briefcase full of papers. Instead of spending time with Jennifer, Daddy spent every evening until way past Jennifer's bedtime, working on those papers.

Finally, Jennifer went to her mother and asked, "Why does Daddy have to do so much work every night?"

"Because," her mother responded, "he doesn't get all of his work done at the office."

Jennifer said, "Couldn't they put him in a slower group?"[1]

If our work is so stressful and overwhelming that we neglect our own family, we may be headed for burnout. Nehemiah has shown us how to prevent burnout. When we are facing a stress overload, we need to take God's advice as offered to us through Nehemiah—and a little girl named Jennifer: We need to put ourselves in a slower group.

Throughout the book of Nehemiah we have seen God use this remarkable man, the cupbearer to the king of Persia, to restore true faith and authentic worship to the land of Judah. Through his example, we also see how to restore true faith and authentic worship to our own lives today.

As we come to the account of Nehemiah's reforms following his second return from Babylon to Jerusalem, you might wonder, "What does this ancient man, who lived centuries before Christ, have to say to my busy life in the twenty-first century?" I think you will see that this account has amazing applicability to your own life today.

Among the hidden hindrances in our lives—factors that prevent us from experiencing the close relationship with God we were meant to have—are our busy-ness, our workaholism, and our lack of downtime and genuine rest. Nehemiah points us to God's solution to the crisis of stress and burnout.

Upon returning to Jerusalem, Nehemiah went all around the city, from the marketplace to the countryside, to see what had changed while he was away. He described all that he saw:

In those days I saw people in Judah treading winepresses on the Sabbath and bringing in grain and loading it on donkeys, together with wine, grapes, figs and all other kinds of loads. And they were bringing all this into Jerusalem on the Sabbath. Therefore I warned them against selling food on that day. People from Tyre who lived in Jerusalem were bringing in fish and all kinds of merchandise and selling them in Jerusalem on the Sabbath to the people of Judah. I rebuked the nobles of Judah and said to them, "What is this wicked thing you are doing—desecrating the Sabbath day? Didn't your ancestors do the same things, so that our God brought all this calamity on us and on this city? Now you are stirring up more wrath against Israel by desecrating the Sabbath." (Nehemiah 13:15–18)

The laws of the Sabbath are still observed in Israel today, by both observant and non-observant Jews. According to these laws, it is forbidden to do work on the Sabbath, to switch electricity on and off, to travel in vehicles, and to cook food. The Sabbath is a day of rest and spiritual contemplation, a time of spending time with family and friends. Stores, restaurants, and the bus lines shut down for the Sabbath.

If you are staying in an Israeli hotel on the Sabbath, you cannot press an elevator button and ride the elevator to a specified floor—that involves pressing an electric switch. You will either have to take the stairs or, in some hotels, take a "Shabbat elevator" that travels automatically from floor to floor, stopping for a minute before moving on. Shabbat elevators have no button to press and are a very slow way to move from floor to floor.

Many non-observant Jews dislike having to observe the Sabbath, but orthodox Jewish groups have sufficient influence to require the entire country to observe the Sabbath day. The Sabbath rules are in force from sundown on Friday until sundown on Saturday.

Even in Nehemiah's time, this was a burdensome requirement for many people. It meant that no work could be done, and no business could be carried out for a full day. If you cannot work, if you cannot run your business, you cannot make money. So, after Nehemiah left Jerusalem, people gradually began to chip away at the Sabbath day requirements until the Sabbath became just like any other day in Israel. The streets were full of traffic and the marketplace was full of wares to be sold.

Nehemiah was away from Jerusalem for twelve years. A lot can happen in twelve years. Just twelve short years after the Wright Brothers invented powered flight, aerial dogfights and bombardment helped determine the outcome of World War I. It was twelve years from the launch of the first satellite, Sputnik, to the landing of the first man on the moon. And it was twelve years from the collapse of the Berlin wall to the terror attacks of 9/11. Similarly, Nehemiah was shocked to see all the changes that had taken place in Judah during his twelve-year absence.

The people had forgotten the lessons of the past. They had forgotten their vow to keep God's law. They had forgotten what a serious thing it is to ignore God's regulations for a healthy and happy life. So Nehemiah said to the people, in effect, "What are you doing? Don't you know that God takes the Sabbath seriously? We have gone through a national tragedy of captivity and slavery because our forefathers failed to observe God's law—and now you are following in their footsteps."

God's Stress Management Program

By his authority as governor of the province of Judah, Nehemiah immediately began making changes:

> When evening shadows fell on the gates of Jerusalem before the Sabbath, I ordered the doors to be shut and not opened until the Sabbath was over. I stationed some of my own men at the gates so that no load could be brought in on the Sabbath day. Once or twice the merchants and sellers of all kinds of goods spent the night outside Jerusalem. But I warned them and said, "Why do you spend the night by the wall? If you do this again, I will arrest you." From that time on they no longer came on the Sabbath. Then I commanded the Levites to purify themselves and go and guard the gates in order to keep the Sabbath day holy. (Nehemiah 13:19–22)

Nehemiah was angered and offended by the people's disregard for God's law. He ordered the gates be closed at sunset on Friday. He gave stern orders to those who camped outside the walls, waiting for the regulations to be ended so they could begin selling. He told them to stay away from the city walls—or face arrest. He required the Levites to ceremonially purify themselves and stand guard at the gates so no one would violate the Sabbath.

Then he offered another prayer, similar to the prayer of verse 14: "Remember me for this also, my God, and show mercy to me according to your great love" (Nehemiah 13:22).

What do these actions mean for us today? What can we learn from Nehemiah's example that we can apply in our own time, our own culture? Should we also keep the Sabbath by refraining from work, travel, and doing business? Some Christians think so.

Seventh Day Adventists think that it is wrong to celebrate Sunday as the Lord's Day. They claim that Saturday ought to be observed as the Sabbath, and we should hold church services that day, refrain from work, and observe the Sabbath restrictions of the law of Moses. But the apostle Paul clearly tells us: "Therefore do not let anyone judge you by what you eat or drink, or with regard to a religious festival, a New Moon celebration or a Sabbath day. These are a shadow of the things that were to come; the reality, however, is found in Christ" (Colossians 2:16–17).

The Old Testament restrictions were shadows—pictures of a far more important reality that God wants us to understand. He was teaching us, by means of these pictures and shadows, what the Sabbath actually represents. At the heart of the Sabbath is the word *rest*. God intended that the Sabbath should teach us how to rest.

At this point, we begin to see how the ancient laws of God apply to our twenty-first century problems of stress and burnout. We are a restless people. One of the biggest social problems in Silicon Valley, where our church is located, is the stress-related problem of burnout. People become so committed to their careers, to success, to achievement, and to status and wealth that they have no time in their lives to actually live. They have no time for family. They have no time for spiritual reflection and worship. They have no time for rest.

I once heard of a man who went to the airline reservation desk and said, "Give me a ticket." The desk clerk said, "A ticket to where?" He replied, "Anywhere. I've got business everywhere." That's the kind of pressure people are living under these days.

One of the qualities we have lost as a result of our high-pressure, stress-filled way of living is our curiosity about life. We've lost our sense of wonder, our ability to look up and appreciate the night sky, or to simply enjoy the natural wonders of the seashore or the mountains. We have to take our smart phones and laptop computers with us, because we don't dare unplug from the office, the Internet, or social media for even one day. Instead of enjoying those beautiful one-of-a-kind moments with our children, our loved ones, or God himself, we stare at our phones like addicts.

The late architect Frank Lloyd Wright recalled a day when he was nine years old, walking across a snow-covered field with his uncle. Wright's uncle was a rather dour and practical man with an all-business attitude. As the boy and his uncle reached the far end of the snow-covered field, the uncle stopped and pointed backwards.

"Young man," the uncle said, "look at your tracks in the snow. See how they wander aimlessly from the fence to those cattle, to those trees, and back again? Now look at my tracks. See how they run straight as an arrow from there to here? I walked straight to my destination while you wasted time and footsteps wandering all around. There's an important lesson in this that I hope you'll always remember."

The boy did remember. Frank Lloyd Wright recalled that his uncle's words helped shape his philosophy of living—but not in the way the uncle expected. "I determined right then," Wright said, "not to miss most things in life as my uncle had."[2]

God never intended for us to only walk in straight lines. Life is not lived in straight lines. God intended that we should enjoy the journey as well as the destination. That means we need to be a little less driven and a lot less stressed. God intended that we should make time along the way to rest, to reflect, to let our thoughts roam freely, to recover from the pressure and catch up with ourselves. The Sabbath is God's solution to overwork and burnout, so we would not fall apart and become emotionally damaged.

The first thing God emphasized when he gave us the Sabbath was that human beings need rest. Our bodies need rest and our minds need rest. Most important of all, our spirits need rest. We cannot keep working day after day without exacting a toll on ourselves—body and soul. Though our spirits are redeemed, our bodies are mortal and they grow weary.

Two Kinds of Sabbath Rest

I once spent a week at Dallas Theological Seminary, and my speaking schedule was very crowded. In fact, I spoke sixteen times in four days. On one day alone, I spoke to six different audiences, ending with a large home Bible study in Fort Worth. At the end of those four days, I was exhausted, mentally and physically. It is stressful to speak before an audience, and the stress is multiplied when you have to give multiple speeches in one day. Even though God has called me to preach and teach, and even though I enjoy the work God has called me to, there is still an element of stress involved whenever I get up to speak.

At the end of that week, I came home and preached on Sunday morning—and my sermon was about the Sabbath rest. When I finished preaching that day, I truly looked forward to my own "Sabbath" rest—which for me would take place on Monday.

According to the Word of God, we human beings need one day out of seven to rest. The body, mind, and emotions need a time of quiet refreshment. People who fail to heed God's prescription for a healthy life run the risk of making themselves unhappy, unpleasant to be around, and even physically and emotionally sick. That is why God has provided the Sabbath. The Sabbath rest is God's loving provision for our emotional and physical well-being.

The Scriptures give us two reasons for God's institution of the Sabbath. Most Christians are familiar with the first reason, which is found in Exodus 20:11. There God said to Israel, "For in six days the Lord made the heavens and the earth, the sea, and all that is in them, but he rested on the seventh day. Therefore the LORD blessed the Sabbath day and made it holy."

God finished His work of creation in six days and rested on the seventh day. Now, a question immediately occurs to us: Why did God rest? God is not a man. He does not become physically, mentally, or emotionally tired as we do. Why, then, did God rest after six days labor? Answer: He rested because He was finished with His work. He had done what He intended to do. He had accomplished His objective.

By resting on the seventh day, God showed us that we too must recognize a limit to our work. There is a time to say, "Let's call it a day. I've accomplished enough for now. I'll start fresh again in the morning after I've had time to rest."

The second reason God gave the Sabbath to humanity is often ignored. We find it in Deuteronomy 5:15, where God said to Israel, "Remember that you were slaves in Egypt and that the LORD your God brought you out of there with a mighty hand and an outstretched arm. Therefore the LORD your God has commanded you to observe the Sabbath day."

This is a very different reason from the reason given in Exodus. Here, God says that the people were to rest on the Sabbath in order to reflect on God's love, His redemptive power, and His deliverance of Israel from bondage in Egypt. Israel was not able to deliver itself from Egypt. When the people of Israel came to the Red Sea, they panicked. They didn't know how they would get across the waters to the other side. The Egyptian army was in hot pursuit—and the Israelites believed their situation was hopeless.

But God opened the waters before them. He delivered Israel with a mighty hand and an outstretched arm. So God wanted the people of Israel to take the Sabbath day, the day of rest, and use it to reflect on everything God had done for them.

God gave us two reasons for observing the Sabbath—creation and redemption. There are two forms of rest that correspond to these two reasons. There is the rest that comes from a cessation of work, a pause from our labors. One old hymn reminds us:

> Not the labors of my hands
> Can fulfill thy law's demands;
> Could my zeal no respite know,
> Could my tears forever flow,
> All for sin could not atone;
> Thou must save and thou alone.[3]

I cannot contribute to my own redemption. My good works cannot save me. That is the "rest" that God has given to us through the new creation. We are to stop trusting in our own works and trust instead in the work God has done for us through the Lord Jesus Christ. He must save and He alone.

There is also the Sabbath rest that we experience as we rejoice in the mighty power of God. Our deliverance is not an event—it's a process. Many Christians experience salvation as a single moment in time, and they can forever point back to the day, or even the moment, when they were saved. Yet our deliverance is also a daily process of sanctification—of becoming more and more like Christ. And this sanctification process, far from being a heavy burden, is a restful experience of growing in Christ.

In the Gospels, Jesus speaks of these two kinds of Sabbath rests that we experience as we place our faith in Him and grow in Him: "Come to me, all you who are weary and burdened, and I will give you rest. Take my yoke upon you and learn from me, for I am gentle and humble in heart, and you will find rest for your souls. For my yoke is easy and my burden is light" (Matthew 11:28–30).

The first form of Sabbath rest Jesus speaks of here is the rest of regeneration—the rest we experience when we become a new creation. If you are weary and burdened, he says, "Come to me. Trust in me. Rest in what I have already done, and I will give you true rest from your burdens." This is the rest Jesus gives to us.

The second form of Sabbath rest Jesus speaks of here is the rest we find as we walk with the Lord and grow in Him. Jesus uses a metaphor to describe this form of rest—a yoke. A yoke was a device that bound two oxen together at the neck so they would work together as one. Jesus said that once we become yoked with Him, we begin to walk in step with Him and learn from Him—and in the process, we find rest for our souls. Why? Because His yoke is easy, and His burden is light. The first form of Sabbath rest Jesus spoke of is the regeneration He gives us; but the second form of Sabbath rest is the rest that we find as we walk with the Lord.

Both forms of rest are symbolized in the Old Testament commands regarding the Sabbath. The Old Testament Sabbath law is a picture of the Sabbath rest Jesus gave to us in the New Testament. The Sabbath law said to people of Israel—and to people of all cultures in all times: Stop trying to save yourself.

We are to trust in the work of Jesus the Messiah. We are to hear Him, obey Him, be joined and yoked with Him, walk with Him throughout our life, and find our Sabbath rest in Him.

We hear about these blessed rests in our churches, we sing about them in our hymns, but we seldom observe these rests in our daily lives. Instead of finding rest for our souls in Christ, we seek our rest from outside sources such as secular advice or even things like alcohol. We ignore what Jesus himself has offered us.

We have a High Priest, the New Testament tells us, who empathizes with our weakness, who has been tempted as we are (yet without sin), enabling us to "approach God's throne of grace with confidence, so that we may receive mercy and find grace to help us in our time of need" (see Hebrews 4:15–16). That High Priest is none other than Jesus himself. Yet few of us actually rely on the provision of strength, grace, and rest that He offers us to relieve the pressures and burdens of our lives.

Drawing from an Inexhaustible Supply

I hope you see now why I call the Sabbath "God's stress management program." Burnout is the result of overstress. It's the result of a lack of rest in our lives—whether we are speaking of physical rest, emotional rest, or spiritual rest. If we do not stop and rest, if we do not allow God to relieve the burdens we carry on a daily basis, the result will be physical, emotional, and/or spiritual burnout.

The symptoms of burnout vary from person to person. My symptoms may be very different from yours. Typically, those symptoms may include fatigue (a lack of energy), insomnia, impaired memory, impaired concentration and attention, being prone to illness and other physical symptoms, loss of appetite, poor digestion, anxiety, and depression. Heed these symptoms and consider them warning signs. The human spirit, the center of our being, requires quiet time for contemplation, reflection, and meditation. We need to pull back from our focus on details and activities and schedules. We need to pause and look at the big picture of our lives.

We each need to become aware of the physical, emotional, and spiritual symptoms we encounter when we become over-stressed. It took me years to recognize the stress symptoms in my own life. Once I learned to recognize the signs, I also trained myself to pause and take what I call "a mini-Sabbath."

Whenever I felt pressured, I tried to set aside a half-hour to be alone with God—and I found that this was frequently all the time I needed. I started by taking ten deep breaths to relax my physical being. During this time of deep breathing, I prayed and asked God to speak to me during the next half-hour. I thought about my life during the previous week or several weeks. I asked myself, "How much have I been driven from one crisis to the next, one obligation to the next, one meeting to the next? How many times have I simply rested in God, trusting him to relieve me of my burdens?"

Sometimes, I wrote down the commitments and obligations that were truly important. Then, looking at that list, I asked myself, "If I only had one month to live, how would I spend my time? Would I still spend it on these so-called 'priorities'? And if the answer was no, do they truly deserve to be called 'priorities'?"

This exercise put all my pressures and priorities into perspective—an eternal perspective. I began looking at the momentary urgencies and commitments of my life in terms of their importance in the overall scheme of my life. In this way, I began to realize that some things I had been feeling stressed about were really not all that important. This gave me a Sabbath-perspective, and I was able to allow God to relieve me of those stresses and burdens.

I emerged from this brief half-hour of reflection with a new outlook—and I realized that many of the issues I had been stressing

over actually evaporated. I didn't feel tʰ
I absorbed an enormous amount of
thirty minutes. This liberating exe⸍
tive way of implementing God's
my life.

One way of looking at the issue of bu⸍
life as an oil lamp. The lamp gives light becausᵉ ⸍
end of the wick. Yet it is not the wick that burns. ⸍.
strip of porous material (such as cloth) that is dipped dowɴ
reservoir of oil. The wick draws oil up toward the flame, and it ɪꜱ
the oil that burns, not the wick itself. As long as there is oil in the
lamp, the wick will not burn.

But if the lamp runs out of oil, the fire will have no more oil to
burn—and it will begin to burn up the wick itself. This is what
burnout is like in a human life. As long as you live in total dependence on the oil of the Holy Spirit, as long as you maintain a steady
supply of His power, you are like that wick—burning brightly, giving
off light and heat, but without being consumed. But if you cease
to draw upon God's supply for your life, the combustion of life's
problems and pressures will ultimately leave you burned out—your
physical and spiritual energy expended.

Keep drawing on His supply for your life. Let His power flow
in you, let His light shine through you. God has a limitless supply
of light and power. Let Him be your source, your supply, and your
Sabbath rest, and you will never burn out.

In This Dying World, Not of It

The final problem Nehemiah faced was Israel's failure to obey
the prohibition against intermarriage with pagan people. Upon
returning to Jerusalem after his long absence, he found the people
disobeying the very law they had sworn, in writing, to obey:

n those days I saw men of Judah who had married women
dod, Ammon and Moab. Half of their children spoke the
e of Ashdod or the language of one of the other peoples,
d not know how to speak the language of Judah. (Nehemiah
23–24)

It has always been true that when the fathers disobey, it is the
children who suffer. Children were being born in Israel who did
not know the Jewish language—and if they didn't know how to
communicate in the language of Judah, you can be sure they were
also not learning the Jewish culture, traditions, and faith. They were
being brought up according to the language, culture, and religious
practices of the pagans.

The parallel between these events and the Christian church today
is unmistakable. When Christians begin to adopt the values and
ways of the surrounding culture, the children grow up not knowing what biblical values and biblical traditions are. In the process,
we are turning our children away from the very beliefs and values
upon which to build a strong and stable family life—and a righteous nation.

A number of years ago, I had a conversation with a man who
had been the pastor of a large evangelical church. The church board
became dominated by elders who came from a business background.
They decided they wanted to run the church like a business, and
they ignored much of what the New Testament says about the way
elders are to function as shepherds of God's flock. They introduced
secular structures and decision-making processes, and they elected
a board chairman who would act as a CEO with power to dictate
even to the pastor.

The pastor had been teaching expositional messages through the
Scriptures—that is, taking a book of the Bible and teaching straight
through it, from beginning to end, instead of cherry-picking favorite

themes and avoiding unpleasant subjects. The church's chairman and the board told the pastor he must stop preaching with an expositional method. They said it was taking too long to get through certain books of the Bible, and the pastor often preached on subjects the board members didn't want to hear about. The pastor insisted that he would preach the full counsel of God. So the board fired this pastor and replaced him with a minister who would obey the church bosses.

The pastor told me about these events with tears running down his face—not tears of self-pity that he had been fired, but tears of sorrow for the flock he was leaving behind. He said that he knew of many individuals, especially young people, who had left the church is a result of these changes—and some had wandered from the faith.

This is what happens when we import the world's values and processes into the church. God designed His church to operate on His principles, just as He designed the nation of Israel to operate on the laws He set forth. Whenever Israel departed—and whenever the church departs—from God's original blueprint, the result is disaster. That is why Nehemiah was grieved and angered by Israel's rapid descent into apostasy during his absence. And that is why he immediately took drastic action:

> I rebuked them and called curses down on them. I beat some of the men and pulled out their hair. I made them take an oath in God's name and said: "You are not to give your daughters in marriage to their sons, nor are you to take their daughters in marriage for your sons or for yourselves. Was it not because of marriages like these that Solomon king of Israel sinned? Among the many nations there was no king like him. He was loved by his God, and God made him king over all Israel, but even he was led into sin by foreign women. Must we hear now that you too are doing all this terrible wickedness and are being unfaithful to our God by marrying foreign women?"

One of the sons of Joiada son of Eliashib the high priest was son-in-law to Sanballat the Horonite. And I drove him away from me. (Nehemiah 13:25–28)

As we saw in the previous chapter, we need to be careful with accounts of events in the Old and New Testaments. This account in Nehemiah 13, like the account of the cleansing of the temple by Jesus, should not be viewed as a model for our behavior today. Nehemiah was acting in his official capacity as governor of the province of Judah. Jesus was acting in His anointed capacity as the Messiah of Israel. You and I do not have the perfect wisdom that Jesus exhibited to mete out just the right balance of righteousness and indignation. Our anger all too easily flies out of control—and human anger tends to magnify the problems it seeks to address.

We must never forget that the actions we see in the Old Testament are shadows of New Testament realities. God does not expect us to follow the actions of Nehemiah as a literal blueprint. What Nehemiah does here in addressing the apostasy of Israel is a picture of a far more important reality that God wants us to understand. He wants us to move beyond the external teaching mechanism of the shadows to the meaning that these shadows portray. We are to follow the fulfillment of the shadow, not the shadow itself.

Here, Nehemiah portrays commendable zeal in acting decisively against the practice of intermarrying with pagans. He drove away the grandson of the high priest who had married the daughter of Sanballat the Horonite, a worshipper of the god Horon who had opposed God's work from the beginning. What should we learn from this Old Testament shadow?

This account illustrates the foolishness of trying to merge the ways of God with the ways of this fallen and dying world. That is what the folly of intermarriage with pagans portrays for us today. The issue is not racial or ethnic. The issue is spiritual. Those who would import the business philosophies and ethical philosophies of the world into the Lord's church are engaging in the same sin and self-delusion that destroyed the legacy of King Solomon. God's work must be done God's way.

In the closing verses of this chapter, Nehemiah prays:

> Remember them, my God, because they defiled the priestly office and the covenant of the priesthood and of the Levites. So I purified the priests and the Levites of everything foreign, and assigned them duties, each to his own task. I also made provision for contributions of wood at designated times, and for the firstfruits. Remember me with favor, my God. (Nehemiah 13:29–31)

These are some of the saddest words in Scripture: "because they defiled the priestly office and the covenant of the priesthood and of the Levites." God created the priestly office to be a picture of the ministry of Jesus Christ. He is the great High Priest who would come to meet us in our lostness and weakness, and restore us to a right relationship with God the Father. The church, the body of Christ, is called to the same work, the same ministry. So these priests of Nehemiah's day didn't merely betray their priestly calling and profession in that day. They betrayed the picture of what God was doing from the beginning to the end of history through Jesus the Messiah, our High Priest.

Jesus himself defined the work of the church for us in that wonderful scene in the synagogue of Nazareth where he quoted these words from the book of Isaiah:

> "The Spirit of the Lord is on me,
>   because he has anointed me
>   to proclaim good news to the poor.
> He has sent me to proclaim freedom for the prisoners
>   and recovery of sight for the blind,

to set the oppressed free,
        to proclaim the year of the Lord's favor." (Luke 4:18–19)

That is the work of the church: to preach the good news of the gospel, to minister to hurting people, to lift the burden of sin and guilt from their lives, to liberate them from oppression, to lead them out of their spiritual blindness and into the light of freedom and hope. That is the work of the church—and the work of the church always suffers when we replace God's principles with the fallen principles of this world.

We are in this world, but we are not of this world. We are like the scuba diver who is in the ocean but not of the ocean. The air he breathes is the air he has taken with him from the world above. If he were try to breathe in the environment that surrounds him, he would drown.

We are like the astronaut who is in airless space but not of airless space. The air he breathes is the air he has brought with him from his home world. If he were to step into outer space and pop open his space helmet and try to breathe in that airless environment, he would suffocate.

Some time ago, a firefighter stood on the roof of a burning home, cutting through the roof with his ax to ventilate it—when the roof collapsed and he fell inside. Flames billowed up from the hole in the roof. The firefighter was trapped in the inferno. It took a couple of minutes for his fellow firefighters to get into the house, locate him, and pull him out of the flames. He suffered extensive burns and was hospitalized in critical condition—but he survived and was eventually able to return home to his family.

How did he survive at least two full minutes in that fire? Well, when he fell, he was wearing protective clothing: a mask that shielded his face, and an air tank that enabled him to breathe even though he was immersed in an environment of fire and smoke. He was in the fire, but he was protected from death because he carried the cool, sweet, life-giving air of his home world into that deadly furnace.

When we go into the world, we must be like that scuba diver, that astronaut, that firefighter. We must be in this world of death but not of it. It is deadly to bring the environment of this dying world into our souls, into our churches, and into our faith. The pagan beliefs and ungodly values of this dying world do not mix with God's blueprint, God's people, or God's church.

This present world is not our home. We long for a better world, a better country—a heavenly and eternal land. So while we are in this world, let us breathe the air of our true home. Let us think the thoughts of our true home. Let us embrace the ways and the values of our true home.

That is, I believe, the most important lesson of the book of Nehemiah for your life and mine. God has placed us here to change the world, not to conform to it. May we walk honorably before God as Nehemiah did, praying as he prayed, "Remember me with favor, my God."

And may we one day hear, when we take our first breath in our everlasting home, "Well done, good and faithful servant! Come and share your Master's happiness!"

NOTES

Chapter 1: A Plan for Rebuilding—and Succeeding

1. Kate Bowler, "Sunday Review: Death, the Prosperity Gospel and Me," *New York Times*, February 13, 2016, Web.

2. Jonathan Aitken, *John Newton: From Disgrace to Amazing Grace* (Wheaton, IL: Crossway, 2007), 125.

3. Aitken, 126.

4. T. S. Grimshawe, *The Works of William Cowper: His Life, Letters, and Poems* (Boston: Crosby, Nichols, Lee & Co., 1860), 659.

5. John Newton, *Thoughts Upon the African Slave Trade*, Samuel J. May Anti-Slavery Collection, Carl A. Kroch Library, Cornell University.

Chapter 2: Don't Despair—Begin to Repair

1. Marc Fisher, "Clinton's Pastor with a Past," *Washington Post*, September 28, 1998, Web.

2. Gordon MacDonald, *Rebuilding Your Broken World* (Nashville: Thomas Nelson, 2003), 185.

Chapter 4: Don't Be Paralyzed—Get Organized!

1. David Nicholls, *One Day* (New York: Vintage Books, 2009), 4.

2. Isaac Watts (1674–1748), "Am I a Soldier of the Cross," hymn, public domain.

3. Jessie B. Pounds (1861–1921), "The Way of the Cross Leads Home," 1906, hymn, public domain.

Chapter 5: Don't Back Down—Build Up!

1. Martin Luther (1483–1546), "A Mighty Fortress Is Our God," hymn, public domain.

Chapter 6: Don't Vacillate—Perpetuate!

1. David McCullough, *Truman* (New York: Simon & Schuster, 1992), 436.
2. F. B. Meyer, *Our Daily Homily*, Homily 183, Nehemiah 6:3 Christian Classics Ethereal Library.
3. As referred to in the *Aeneid* of Virgil and in Homer's *Odyssey*.
4. Henry David Thoreau, *Walden* (New York: Thomas Y. Crowell & Co., 1910), 430.

Chapter 7: Rediscovering God's Hidden Riches

1. Richard Reeves, "These Are Scary Times throughout Nation," *Ocala Star-Banner*, January 13, 1989, 10A.
2. C. S. Lewis, *The Problem of Pain*, in *The Complete C. S. Lewis Signature Classics* (New York: HarperOne, 2002), 618.
3. Ray Stedman, "What the Bible Means to Me," RayStedman.org, 2010, Web.

Chapter 8: How to Talk to God

1. David M. Walker, *Comeback America: Turning the Country Around and Restoring Fiscal Responsibility* (New York: Random House, 2009), 36–37.
2. Niall Ferguson, "Complexity and Collapse: Empires on the Edge of Chaos," *Foreign Affairs*, published by the Council on Foreign Relations, March/April 2010, Web.
3. Thomas Jefferson, "Letter to William Short," in *Thomas Jefferson: Writings*, edited by Merrill D. Peterson (New York: Library of America, 1994), 1435–1440.
4. C. Maude Battersby, "An Evening Prayer," circa 1911.

Chapter 9: The New Resolve

1. Richard Dawkins, *The God Delusion* (New York: Houghton Mifflin, 2006), 51.
2. Rhonda Howard, "He Has Conquered," The Lord's Church, April 5, 2015, Web.

Chapter 10: The Ways God Works

1. George Matheson (1842–1906), "O Love That Wilt Not Let Me Go," 1882, hymn, public domain.

Chapter 11: The Sound of Rejoicing

1. Friedrich Nietzsche, *Thus Spoke Zarathustra: A Book for All and None*, translated by Walter Kaufmann (New York: Modern Library, 1995), 92.

2. Friedrich Nietzsche, *The Complete Works of Friedrich Nietzsche: Human, All-Too-Human: A Book for Free Spirits*, Part II, translated by Paul V. Cohn (New York: Macmillan, 1913), 54.

3. The term *goody two-shoes* is based on a children's story published in 1765. *The History of Little Goody Two-Shoes* tells the story of a poor but virtuous girl who goes through life with only one shoe. When a kind man gives her a pair of shoes to wear, she is so pleased with her good fortune that she tells everyone she has "two shoes." She lives a humble and virtuous life, and in the end, her virtue is rewarded when she marries a wealthy man.

Chapter 12: Report for Duty

1. Randy Alcorn, *Heaven* (Wheaton, IL: Tyndale, 2004), 23.

2. David Roper, *The Strength of a Man: 50 Devotionals to Help Men Find Their Strength in God* (Grand Rapids: Discovery House, 1989), 9.

Chapter 13: Preventing Burnout and Preserving Power

1. Bill Swindell, *Fathers, Come Home: A Wake-up Call for Busy Dads* (Boys Town, NE: Boys Town Press, 1992), 39.

2. Mark Buchanan, *Your God Is Too Safe: Rediscovering the Wonder of a God You Can't Control* (Colorado Springs, CO: WaterBrook Multnomah, 2001), 102.

3. Augustus Montague Toplady (1740–1778), "Rock of Ages," 1775, hymn, public domain.

Enjoy this book? Help us get the word out!

Share a link to the book or
mention it on social media

Write a review on your blog, on a retailer site,
or on our website (dhp.org)

Pick up another copy to share with someone

Recommend this book for your
church, book club, or small group

Follow Discovery House on
social media and join the discussion

Contact us to share your thoughts:

 @discoveryhouse    @DiscoveryHouse

Discovery House
P.O. Box 3566
Grand Rapids, MI 49501 USA

Phone: 1-800-653-8333
Email: books@dhp.org
Web: dhp.org